Fell's United States Coin Book

The definitive United States coin guide

Eleventh Revised Edition

Roderick P. Hughes

FELL PUBLISHERS, INC.
Hollywood, Florida

International Standard Book Number: 0-8119-0037-1 (hardcover edition)
0-8119-0542-X (paperback edition)

For information address:
Fell Publishers, Inc.
2131 Hollywood Blvd.
Hollywood, FL 33020

Published simultaneously in Canada by Prentice-Hall Canada, Toronto

Manufactured in the United States of America

Contents

Preface to the Revised Edition ix
Introduction xi
    For whom the volume is written xi
1. A Little History 1
2. Coins Used Before and After the Revolution 5
    European and Mexican coins 5
    State issues 6
    Continental coins 7
3. Official and Unofficial U.S. Coinage 11
    Earliest trial issues and regular denominations 11
    Tokens and privately issued coins 12
    Patterns 13
    The Trade Dollar 14
    Confederate coins 14
    Coins of U.S. possessions 14
4. Coin Minting and Design Features 19
    Metal content, weight and fineness 19
    Coin dating 21
    Mint marks 22
    Obverse and reverse 25
        Mottos 25
        Inscriptions 25
        Other devices 26
        Major portraits, places and symbols 26
    Coin relief and high points 28
    Coin edges and milling 29
    How a coin is manufactured 29
    A note on mintage figures 30
    Mint errors 32

5. Determining a Coin's Value...................................35
    Factors determining value 36
        Mintage...36
        Condition 37
        Popularity..42
        Metal Content 42
    Value as a function of
        time and knowledge 47
6. Values of U.S. Minor Coinage...............................49
    Half cents 49
    Cents 50
    Two-cent pieces 57
    Nickel three-cent pieces................................57
    Nickel five-cent pieces 58
7. Values of Silver and Clad Coins 63
    Silver three-cent pieces 63
    Half-dimes 64
    Dimes 65
    Twenty-cent pieces 69
    Quarter dollars 69
    Half dollars 74
    Dollar coins 80
8. Values of Gold Coins 87
    Gold dollars 89
    $2.50 gold pieces 91
    $3.00 gold pieces 93
    $4.00 gold pieces 93
    $5.00 gold pieces 94
    $10.00 gold pieces 96
    $20.00 gold pieces 98
9. Commemorative Coins 101
    Isabella quarter 102
    Commemorative halves 102
    Lafayette dollar 127
    Gold Commemoratives 127
    Commemorative sets 131
10. Other Special Issues 135
    Proof coins and sets 135
    Mint sets..136
    U.S. bullion coins 137
    Medals/Coins 139
11. Where To Find Coins 141

12. Starting a Collection 145
    Some popular ways of collecting. 145
    Basic coin knowledge 147
    Coin supplies and accessories. 147
13. How to Buy Coins. 149
    Coin shops and coin shows 149
    Buying by mail 151
    Mail sales and auctions. 152
    Buying directly from the Mint 153
    Mass-marketed and promoted coins 153
14. How to Sell Coins 155
    A day in the life of a dealer 155
    Appraised value and worth 157
    Selling at auction 157
    Buy ads 158
    Other collectors 159
15. Hobby or Investment 161
    History and aesthetics 161
    History of coin price appreciation. 163
    Coin investment as a hedge. 166
16. Sources of Knowledge 169
    Coin papers and magazines. 169
    Books—general 170
    Books—grading. 170
    Books—specialized. 171
    Books—errors 172
    Books—counterfeits 172
    Books—investing 172
    Newsletters 173
    Professional organizations and associations 173
    Grading and authentication services 174
17. Counterfeit Coins 175
    Biography 177
    Glossary 179

Preface

The prices for this Eleventh Revised Edition were compiled in the winter months of 1987-88. Some prices will undoubtedly be dated by the time this volume reaches print. Inevitably, over the next several years, many prices for coins will have changed, as virtually every coin's price had changed since the 1983 edition was completed.

As a service to our readers, the author will provide yearly up-dates to the pricing portions of the volume. These may be obtained by sending $2.50 to:

Roderick P. Hughes, Ph.D.

Box 3

St. Bonaventure University

St. Bonaventure, NY 14778

The reader should also be aware that, due to the growing interest in the coins of other nations, Frederick Fell Publishers has produced a companion guide entitled, *Fell's International Coin Book*. For a complete catalogue of other titles write to:

Fell Publishers, Inc.

2131 Hollywood Blvd.

Hollywood FL 33020

For help in the preparation of this volume I have many people to thank: Cindy Paino and Sandy Goodliff did a marvelous job with the typing, especially in those drab pricing chapters, St. Bonaventure University whose facilities could certainly have been put to better use, Fred Scicchitano and Fred Marra for their answers to many coin-related questions, and John Bartimole, my editor.

I am indebted to the previous author, Charles J. Andrews, for the fundamental concept of this work. I have also retained many of his own words in Chapters 1-3.

Bowers and Merena Inc. of Wolfeboro, NH, were most helpful in supplying me with the bulk of the photos necessary for a volume such as this. Although one of the largest coin auction houses and dealerships in the country, they did not hesitate when I contacted them for help.

Thanks also to Patty Lindley for additional photos and her advice regarding photo layout.

To Mrs. Fran Funke who first exposed me to the joys of coin collecting, I offer a very tardy "thank you."

Roderick Hughes

Introduction

This little volume is meant to serve two groups of people.

Its intention is to provide beginning collectors with all the basic information and necessities for the appreciation of numismatics and for the building of a collection that may well retain or increase its value.

The middle chapters provide accurate price information on virtually all coins of more than nominal value from half cents to $20 gold pieces.

Chapter 5 is meant to introduce most every relevant consideration for determining the worth of a coin. This section contains an initial discussion of what has come to be the most controversial area of the hobby—grading. The recent emergence of a number of grading and authentication services points up the degree to which even an experienced collector is unwilling to rely on his own expertise.

The vast price differences that can now be found, especially between the higher grades of uncirculated coins, has had a chilling effect on potential buyers, to say nothing of the substantial losses suffered by those who have for one reason or another purchased substantially—or even slightly—overgraded coins.

Later chapters survey the rudiments of coin collecting. Collecting accessories, where and how to acquire and sell coins, and sources for furthering one's knowledge of numismatics are some of the topics discussed.

The second group for whom this volume may be of some help includes non-collectors—those who have come across an occasional coin that looks to be old and valuable. Often it is difficult to get some sense of real value even from friends and relatives who may be to some degree interested in coins. This volume will help non-collectors get a good idea about whether a professional opinion should be sought.

One especially troublesome situation is to find oneself responsible for a collection of a family member. Who to turn to? It seems unwise to trust completely in the judgment of another, whether he is a friend or not, until some idea is gotten concerning values. Even the inadvertent mishandling of moderately priced coins can seriously affect their value.

This volume, therefore, can supply that preliminary opinion *before* wasting the time of a dealer regarding an item that is quite common in collecting circles and appears extraordinary only to the possessor.

1
A Little History

Since this book is concerned with coins, you may well ask first, "What are coins and how did they come to be used?"

As primitive societies developed, society engaged in commercial transactions and some medium of exchange became necessary. Business was first conducted by the barter system or the exchange of tangible goods. Later, many things served as money, such as slaves, cattle, tin, silk, tea, wampum, leather, shells, nails, and other durable objects.

A metallic medium of exchange, easy to handle and carry, was a normal development very early in commerce. At first, metal—copper, silver, or gold—was exchanged by weight. True coinage evolved when pieces of metal were officially stamped to indicate their fineness and weight, and when the users, having sufficient confidence in this official indication on the pieces of metal, gave and accepted them as media of exchange.

The earliest coins were extremely crude. For example, on some coins busts may be facing to one side while the eyes face front, sometimes hair is indicated by dots. The earliest coins are undated and generally bear some national symbol. The style of the workmanship and the symbols on the coin furnish the only clues as to the date. As nearly as we can determine, the first silver coins were made about 700 BC, probably in Aegina, while the Lydians are believed to have been the first coiners of gold. The earliest Asiatic coins were those of Miletus in Ionia, followed by the Persian Daric, which was widely used as money and depicts a kneeling royal archer.

The earliest Greek coins carry representations of plants, fish, birds, animals, or motifs connected with local history or religion. For instance, Macedonian coins show a lion eating a bull. The coins of Athens bear the

1

sacred owl, those of Aegina a sea tortoise. The Minotaur and labyrinth appear on Cretan coins.

The early Greek inventors of coinage recorded some of their history on their coins, and subsequent generations in every country have done the same. The history of a migration to Asia Minor, for example, survives through the seals which are pictured in some coin designs. The ship that made the voyage was followed by a large number of seals, which suggested to the migrants a name for the city they founded in Asia Minor, Phocea, the Greek word for seal.

Besides historic events, objects sacred to certain gods and goddesses inspired coin designs, such as grapes for the god Bacchus and the stag for Diana.

The early Romans made their coins of copper, establishing the standard as a 12-oz. pound of copper. It is interesting that the pictures of animals stamped on these first copper coins gave us the word "pecuniary" from the Latin *pecus,* meaning cattle. Further developments produced coins with more detail, often incorporating human figures. Symbols, however, continued in use, the new ones during this period including things like bees, shields, chariots with horses, birds, and other animals. Later elaborations included portraits of the gods, followed in time by portraits of various kings in Egypt, Bactria, Syria, Sicily, and Syracuse.

Early Indian coins were very simple and resembled small weights. Coins were used in China at a very early date, said to be as early as 1091 BC, in the Chou dynasty. Chinese coins, like modern round pieces, were adopted about 250 BC. They were made with holes so that they could be carried on strings.

About 190 BC many cities began to coin money. The first Jewish coins come from this period. Before that, chunks or pieces of metal alone had been used by weight for commercial exchanges. The first money used in Palestine was Persian, followed by Greek and Egyptian. The word "shekel" means a weight, not coined money. In the year 139 to 138 BC the right of coinage was granted to the Jews by the King of Syria. The coins, inscribed in old Hebrew with the words "Shekel of Israel" and "Jerusalem the Holy," are dated from 1 to 5. Those of the first four years were issued by Simon Maccabee and those of the fifth by his son and successor, John Hycanus. John also issued bronze coins with the name "John, the High Priest," inscribed in Hebrew on them.

Under the early Roman emperors, the coins used in Palestine were Roman. The first revolt, in the reign of Nero, occurred in 66 AD, ending four years later with the destruction of Jerusalem and its temple. Some coins of Vespasian and Titus celebrated the defeat of the Jews. These victory pieces show the defeat on one side and a weeping Jewess on the other. The last Jewish money issued in antiquity appeared during the second revolt, in the reign of Hadrian.

Silver money was first struck in Rome in 268 BC. For more than a century the designs offered little variation, but beginning about 134 BC, the designs began to refer to various persons and events connected with the family history of the Roman rulers.

Very few gold coins were made until after Caesar's death. The coins of the emperors began in 27 BC with Octavius, who became Emperor Augustus after his naval victory at Actium. Roman gold coins were practically the only gold coins in circulation throughout the world until the year 1252. In size and appearance they more nearly resemble modern gold coins than any made before the 16th century.

Succeeding Roman coinage, a series of coins in various countries led to modern coinage. They reflected the conquests, customs, religions, and symbols of these countries. In England, the Roman coins were superseded by Saxon coins, followed, after a long series of rulers, by the coinage of Church officials and ultimately by that of the monarchs of England down to the present day.

In Italy, the Lombards were without coinage until the series by Charlemagne, which was succeeded by the coinage of the independent officials of towns and provinces and by Papal coins. The first coins to begin to replace the Roman ones were issued in Florence in 1252. Venice had begun its own coinage in the 10th century and other cities had followed suit, until, with the unification of Italy, modern Italian coinage developed. Spain, France, Germany, Holland, Russia, Denmark, and other countries repeat this general pattern.

Thus we see that the coins created for everyday use in all ages and all countries actually reflect the pageantry of history. Social and political developments and the individual characteristics of various peoples are illustrated by their coinage. Man's progress from conquest and tyranny, from fear and superstition, through all his disheartening setbacks, is to be read as clearly in his coins as in his written histories. We know equally well that the history of the future, with man's aspirations for brotherhood and peace, will be as plainly shown in the coins to come. Viewed in this light, the collecting of coins can never lose its attraction.

2
U.S. Coins Before and After the Revolution

EUROPEAN AND MEXICAN COINS

To show the variety of coins collectible from this era, I quote from an old treatise on coins, which in the course of 700 pages contains only this reference to American coins: "The money of America does not date back further than the European discovery and occupation in the 16th century, when the Spanish, Portuguese, English, etc., minted money for their colonies, in all cases very similar in character to that of the mother country."

As in all developing countries, the need for coins was felt in America at an early period. At first, the colonists used Indian wampum, collections of shells ground to small size and formed into belts. This type of money had value, not because of the worth of the material, but because of the amount of labor required to produce it. The General Court of Massachusetts on Nov. 15, 1637, decreed that wampum should pass as currency at six for a penny. In 1640, in what must surely be the first devaluation of the New World, the courts established white wampum at 14 for a penny and blue at two for a penny. Recognition of wampum as money was withdrawn in 1661. During this early period, musket balls were also used as currency, valued at about one-half cent apiece.

The earliest coins in America were made in Mexico about 1635. Coins specifically for the American colonies were first made for Somers Islands (Bermuda). The islands were named for Sir George Somers, who was shipwrecked there. These coins were struck in England sometime before 1616.

During this early period European money was circulated in the colonies, particularly French, Dutch, Italian, English, and Spanish, with the same values as in the mother countries but the coins of Spain were most prevalent. Spanish coins were recognized throughout the colonies. In fact, Connecticut, Massachusetts and Virginia passed laws making them legal tender. Until 1857, Spanish money was legally acceptable in trade in the United States. From this money we have obtained one of our most famous colloquialisms, the term "two bits." A Spanish dollar consisted of eight bits, the half dollar of four, and the quarter of two.

STATE ISSUES

The first strictly American coins were made by the General Court of Massachusetts at Boston in 1652 in the denomination of one shilling and sixpence.

From the design of this coin and its crudeness, it is apparent that it could easily be copied or that silver could be clipped from it. Consequently, these coins did not last long. They were replaced first by the Willow Tree shilling and then by the Oak Tree and Pine Tree shilling.

The Oak Tree coins made by the Massachusetts mint were really an exercise of sovereign rights that did not belong to the colonies. However, Charles II was told that the oak tree had been chosen in his honor because this tree had saved his life. He was so pleased with this that he did not object to the coinage.

1652 Pine Tree Shilling

The Pine Tree shilling illustrated here was made for about 30 years, but all coins bear the date 1652. An interesting story connected with this coin is the tale that the mint master who coined this money became very rich and when his daughter married he put her on a scale and gave as a dowry her weight in Pine Tree shillings. Legend has it that she was no featherweight!

Since the reason for the issuance of various silver and copper coins was the need of the colonists for money, occasionally someone in England would cause coins to be issued on speculation and export them to America to be used as currency. An example is the so-called Woods Coinage from 1722 to 1724. This is known as part of the Rosa Americana series.

1722 Woods Hibernia Cent

An initial design was said to have been made for use in Ireland, but it was rejected there and sent to the colonies. The second design was made specifically for the colonies. At about the same time, there were coins for use in Maryland in 1659, Florida in 1685, and Carolina in 1694.

The first copper coins actually made in America were struck by Higley in Connecticut from 1737 to 1739.

In Louisiana, French coins were used, made for the colonies in 1721 and 1722.

CONTINENTAL COINS

Every schoolchild is familiar with the so-called Continental currency, paper money which was used to pay the soldiers during the Revolution. When it became worthless, the saying arose, "I don't give a Continental."

1776 Continental Dollar

However, during the war, in 1776, pattern dollar pieces made of pewter and other metals were also made. These too, I suppose, could be called "Continentals." Part of the inscription actually read "Continental Currency." Specimens in silver and brass are quite rare.

During the Revolutionary War and the years immediately following, many coins were issued, some minted in England for American use and some in America on speculation. That is, if these coins were accepted by the people, the minter would gain a profit because his sole costs were the copper and the cost of minting. Among these coins was the Franklin Penny.

Money in circulation included the Constelatio Cent, the Fugio Cent, and other coins. The Fugio Cent is illustrated below.

Fugio Cent

Before the establishment of the U.S. Mint, a series of Washington pieces was made to honor George Washington. They bear the dates 1783, 1791, 1792, 1793, 1795. An example of these is shown below:

1791 Washington Piece

It is beyond the scope of a work of this kind to give a valuation of colonial money. Many pieces are common and worth a few dollars, while many are extremely rare. Counterfeits and restrikes of practically all of them are known to exist.

Between the Revolution and the establishment of the U.S. Mint, various states authorized coinage and issued coins or imported them from England for their own use. These include:

Massachusetts—1776, 1787 and 1788
Maryland—1788 and 1790
New Jersey—1786-88
Connecticut—1785-88
New Hampshire—1776
Vermont—1785-88
Kentucky—1785 and 1796
New York—1786-87 and 1796

The most publicized of the coins of this period is the Brasher Doubloon, which provided the title of a popular motion picture some years ago. The coin is also celebrated for its extremely high price. In 1907 one of them, made of gold and dated 1787, sold for $6,200. A copy sold in 1979 for $725,000. Only a very few copies exist.

3

Official and Unofficial U.S. Coinage

EARLIEST TRIAL PIECES AND DENOMINATIONS

The United States Congress established a mint in 1786, but the only coin issued by the mint for a number of years was the Fugio Cent described in the previous chapter. This coin was specifically ordered by Congress and no further resolutions for other coins were passed until 1791. This Fugio Cent was struck by private contract since the young government had no actual mint in operation.

In 1791, Congress again resolved that a mint be established and authorized President Washington to proceed with its organization. Accordingly a building was erected and in 1792 a few dimes and half dimes (in those days the spelling was dismes) were struck. It is said that Washington furnished the silver from his own silver plate stock for these coins.

In 1793 work at the mint started in earnest and from then on there was regular coinage. The following is a list of the kinds of coins made by the government and the first year of issue:

Copper half cent	1793	$2.50 gold	1796
Copper cent	1793	$20 gold	1850
Five-cent silver		Three-cent silver	1851
or half dime	1794	$3 gold	1854
Half dollar	1794	Two-cent piece	1864
Silver dollar	1794	Three-cent nickel	1865
$5 gold	1795	Five-cent nickel	1866
$10 gold	1795	Trade dollar	1873
Dime	1796	Twenty-cent piece	1875
Quarter	1796	$4 gold (a pattern)	1879

TOKENS AND PRIVATELY ISSUED COINS

Over the years many items have been issued, more or less officially, that have functioned as legal tender. These include a variety of tokens, encased postage stamps, and private mint issues.

Issued from 1834 to 1841, for example, were a number of political cartoons on coins, referring to the financial troubles current in those years. President Andrew Jackson was in a hot political battle with certain financial interests and since the hard times caused a shortage of copper coins, various tokens were privately struck to be used as money. These, of course, were meant to convey political messages for or against the president. Among the slogans inscribed on the Jackson Cents are:

Millions for defense, not one cent for tribute
Webster-Credit Currency
Substitute for Shin Plaster
Van Buren metallic currency
Specie payment suspended

Besides such tokens as these, of which there were hundreds of kinds, various store cards or advertising pieces were issued from 1789 to 1850. Some of these store cards also circulated as money.

During the War between the States there were thousands of varieties of Civil War tokens. Because of the shortage of regular money, private firms, for convenience and for advertising, issued these coins as pennies. They continued to circulate and were valid until 1867.

At about this same period, postage stamps, encased in brass with a mica window, were also used as change. The back of the brass bore an advertisement of the issuing company, such as:

Take Ayer's Pills
Dougan the Hatter
Evans California Wines
Lord and Taylor
North American Life Insurance Company
John Shillito and Company

During the Gold Rush, there was a shortage of coins in California because the government would not accept gold dust in payment of taxes. As a result, speculators sold gold coins at a premium, though even this supply fell short of the demand. Consequently, gold pieces were issued by the following companies or persons in various denominations:

Humbert	Templeton Reid
Wass Molitor	Baldwin and Co.
Kellogg and Co.	Moffat and Co.
Kohler and Co.	Cincinnati Mining
Pacific Company	Schultz and Co.
Dubosq and Co.	Dunbar and Co.
Miners Bank	Clark, Gruber and Co.
J.S. Ormsby	J.J. Conway
Mass. and Calif. Co.	Parsons
Norris, Grieg and Norris	Mormon Gold (Utah)
C. Bechtler	Oregon Exchange Co.
A. Bechtler	U.S. Assay Office

All such gold coins have considerable value. The Humbert $50 Piece, for example, can sell for $5,000 and up. Most familiar to the general public are the California gold pieces.

These were tokens issued with the following denominations and dates:

25 cents	(round and octagonal)	1853-80
50 cents	(round and octagonal)	1852-78
$1	(round and octagonal)	1853-76

Copies of these were made in gold and in brass. An easy way to tell the difference is that most of the genuine pieces bear an inscription of their value, for example, "1/4 Dol." or "Dollar." The imitations omit the word "dollar." Genuine pieces sell anywhere from $65 to $2,000.

PATTERNS

Also, existing in small quantities are a series of designs on coins called patterns. These represent suggested coin designs, some of which were later adopted, or they may be actual trial pieces struck from accepted designs and tested in various metals. Sometimes they were struck as samples to see what the final coin would look like if the design were adopted.

Most of these were prepared by the official engravers of the United States Mint. The accepted designs were those approved by Congress, not necessarily those with the most artistic merit. This series is collected by specialists, with two exceptions which have become so popular that they are collected by the ordinary collector as well—the Flying Eagle cent of 1856 and the $4 gold piece of 1879 and 1880. The quantity of patterns is very limited, since usually only one to 500 pieces were struck. For that reason the pieces tend to be quite valuable.

THE TRADE DOLLAR

You may have noticed in the list of United States coins the Trade Dollar, first minted in 1873. This is the only U.S. money that is no longer valid as legal tender. It was minted to compete with the Mexican dollars and others of high silver content. It contains slightly more silver than the Mexican dollar and somewhat more (7.5 grains) than the regular U.S. dollar. Intended to facilitate trade with China, many of them are marked with Chinese characters stamped on them by the Chinese bankers.

CONFEDERATE COINS

During the War between the States, the Confederacy initiated coinage, issuing two pieces which were never actually used. The Confederate cent was struck as a sample and the Confederate half dollar was prepared and four pieces struck. A lack of silver bullion prevented the continued coinage of the half dollars and the dies were confiscated. These dies turned up years later and from them several hundred coins were made on the reverses of U.S. half dollars of 1861. These restruck copies are worth about $700 in circulated condition.

During the war, the people of the South gave the Confederacy their bullion in silver and gold, receiving in return Confederate paper money of various denominations from $1-$1000. This money was issued from 1861 to 1864 in enormous quantities, and, because of the fortunes of war, became worthless.

Printed by the government of the Confederacy, this money depicted scenes and persons associated with the Southern cause.

Jefferson Davis, president of the Confederacy, Mrs. Davis, Stonewall Jackson, Blacks loading cotton, and similar subjects can be found on these pieces.

In addition to the paper issued by the Confederate government, millions of dollars' worth of paper were issued by individual states: Alabama, Arkansas, Florida, Georgia, Louisiana, Mississippi, Missouri, North Carolina, South Carolina, Texas and Virginia.

All of this paper is worthless as legal tender and relatively cheap from a collector's point of view. A very few of the bills are rare enough to be worth $50 or more, but the majority can be bought from a coin dealer for much less.

COINS OF THE U.S. POSSESSIONS

In addition to the U.S. coins described elsewhere in this volume, you may be interested in collecting coins of the American territories and dependencies. Those whose coinage is of interest to collectors include Puerto Rico, the Virgin Islands, Hawaii and the Philippines.

Puerto Rico

Puerto Rico, discovered by Columbus, is the easternmost island of the Greater Antilles group in the West Indies. The United States acquired it in 1898 by paying $20 million to Spain on that country's relinquishment of all claims to Puerto Rico, Guam, and the Philippine Islands. The Organic Act of Puerto Rico, passed in 1917, granted to Puerto Ricans American citizenship and unrestricted suffrage.

A number of damaged U.S. coins, counterstamped rather crudely with the fleur-de-lys, circulated in Puerto Rico after 1884:

U.S. twenty-cent piece (1875-1878)	Fine*	$400.00
U.S. quarter dollar (1866-1891)	Fine	125.00
U.S. half dollar (1839-1866)	Fine	130.00
U.S. Bust dollar (1798-1803)	Fine	200.00
U.S. Trade dollar (1873-1885)	Fine	200.00

Some Spanish coins were counterstamped in much the same fashion, but more commonly, while the island was under Spanish domain, coins were issued by the Spanish government specifically for use in the colony. With the dates of issue and their present-day retail values, they are:

1 peso	Silver	1895	$300.00
40 centavos	Silver	1895	225.00
20 centavos	Silver	1895	35.00
10 centavos	Silver	1896	30.00
5 centavos	Silver	1896	20.00

All of these, naturally, became obsolete when the United States took possession of Puerto Rico after the Spanish-American War. Since then United States currency has been used there.

The Virgin Islands

The Virgin Islands, consisting of the Islands of St. Croix, St. Thomas, and St. John, were bought by the United States from Denmark for $25 million in 1917. They are administered by the Department of the Interior. Natives of the Virgin Islands are American citizens with the right to vote if they can read and write the English language.

Countermarked U.S. coins exist, stamped with Frederick VII's monogram, in denominations of half cent, cent, quarter dollar, half dollar and dollar. All are quite rare and counterfeits exist.

When the islands belonged to Denmark they were called the Danish West Indies. Denmark apparently considered them a part of the American continent, however, for some of the coins issued for the islands bear the inscription *Dansk Amerikansk*.

The coins issued during the Danish rule are for the most part moderately priced and may be bought for from $15 to $20 each in fine condition. They are easily identified because they are inscribed either *Dansk Amerikansk* or *Dansk Vest Indien*. There are several designs, and the coins bear the names of different Danish kings.

Upon their purchase by the United States, the islands were given their present name and U.S. currency became the medium of exchange.

Hawaii

Hawaii was an island kingdom when it was discovered by Captain Cook in 1778 and became a constitutional monarchy in 1840. Following a revolution in 1893, a republic was proclaimed that year. By voluntary action of its people, Hawaii ceded its sovereignty to the United States in 1898 and was organized as a Territory two years later.

A short series of coins was issued in Hawaii during the last century. A one-cent piece was minted in 1847 during the reign of King Kamehameha III. This can be purchased today for $200.

Hawaiian Cent

In 1883, during the rule of King Kalakaua I, a series was struck at the San Francisco mint for the government of Hawaii. It consisted of a dime, a quarter, a half dollar and a silver dollar. In fine condition, the set sells for about $275.

The Philippine Islands

Discovered by Magellan in 1521 and conquered by Spain in 1565, the Philippine Islands were ceded to the United States in 1898 by the Treaty of Paris following the Spanish-American War. They achieved complete independence on July 4, 1946, when the United States formally surrendered all rights of possession, supervision, jurisdiction, control, or sovereignty over the territory and the people of the islands. This marked the end of a 12-year transitional period provided by the Tydings-McDuffie Act.

Philippine coinage falls into three series: Filipinas coins issued during the Spanish rule; coins issued by the United States at the Philadelphia, San Francisco, and Manila mints; and coins issued since 1934.

The Spanish coins were of two types: those issued specifically for the Philippines, and countermarked coins (coins with an extra impression added to show they were made for use in the colony). Some of them are very rare.

What follows is a list of the Spanish rulers, with the denominations of coins issued during their reigns:

Charles IV	(1788-1808)	1 quarto
Ferdinand VII	(1808,	1 and 2 quartos
	1814-1833)	1 octavo
Isabella II	(1833-1868)	2 and 4 quartos
		10, 20, and 50 centimos
		1, 2, and 4 pesos in gold
Alfonso XII	(1874-1885)	10, 20, and 50 centimos
		4 pesos in gold
Alfonso XIII	(1886-1898)	1 peso

In addition, countermarked coins were issued with the following marks: MR, Manila, F. 7-degree, Y. II. Pattern coins or trial pieces also exist.

Among the coins issued during the United States rule, those made at Philadelphia have no mint mark. Those made at San Francisco have the mint mark S and those minted in Manila have the mint mark M.

The United States coins were issued from 1903 to 1936 with little change in design. Prices for some representative samples in XF* condition include:

1 peso	Silver (1907-12)	$10.00
50 centavos	Silver (1907-21)	7.50
20 centavos	Silver (1907-29)	2.50
10 centavos	Silver (1907-35)	2.50
5 centavos	Copper-Nickel	1.00
1 centavo	Bronze	1.00
½ centavo	Bronze	1.00

When the islands became the Republic of the Philippines in 1934, the government instituted new coinage with coins struck at Manila, Denver, San Francisco, and Philadelphia. To celebrate their new estate, and in friendship for the United States, the government selected designs for the first silver issues which bore the likenesses of Franklin D. Roosevelt, Governor General of the Philippines Frank Murphy, and Manuel Quezon, first president of the Republic of the Philippines.

This series includes a 50-centavos piece issued in 1936, showing Quezon and Murphy, which is now worth $20 in VF*. Others are one-peso pieces issued in the same year, one type carrying the portraits of Roosevelt and Quezon, the other Murphy and Quezon. These may now be had for $6 each in VF.

In 1947 two coins were issued by the Philippines honoring General Douglas MacArthur, and bearing his likeness. They were half-peso and peso pieces. The pair can be bought for $25.

Other commemorative coins of one-peso denomination have been struck in silver, bearing the dates 1961, 1963, 1964, 1967 and 1969. These range in value from $5 to $10, from fine to uncirculated condition. A commemorative coin celebrating the visit of Pope Paul VI, dated 1970, was minted in nickel, silver and gold. These coins bring as high as $2.50, $10 and $500, respectively, in uncirculated condition.

*See Chapter 5 for a discussion of the grading of coins.

4
Coin Minting and Design Features

That handful of change in your pocket or purse can reveal a great deal of information about the "hows" and "wheres" and "what fors" of coin minting and design. Let us look at a few.

METAL CONTENT, WEIGHT AND FINENESS

The color of a coin is as good an indication as any of its composition. U.S. cents have traditionally been made of copper, although the content and amount of the metal has varied considerably over the years. The original Large cents 1793-1857 were made entirely of copper and were approximately the size of the half dollar.

Since the end of the Large cent era, the one-cent coin has been alloyed from time to time with nickel, zinc and tin. In 1943, due to the need for copper in the war effort, the cent was made of steel with a zinc coating. Since 1982, although the color of the cent does not vary much from previous years since it is still copper coated, the composition was changed to 97.5% zinc and 2.5% copper.

Two other copper coins are the half cent (100%) and the two-cent piece (95%).

All our "nickel" coins, including the "nickel" three-cent piece, are somewhat misnamed as they are 75% copper and only 25% nickel.

The only exception to the above is found in the war years (1942-1945) when the composition of the five-cent piece was changed to 56% copper, 35% silver and 9% manganese. The color of the circulated nickels is a dull gray, albeit a darker cast for the wartime alloys.

Generally, our silver coins have contained 90% of the white metal alloyed with 10% copper. From 1965-1970 the composition of the Kennedy half dollar was changed to 40% silver and 60% copper. This same composition is found in proof dollars (1971-1974) and for some bicentennial quarters, half dollars and dollars.

However, with these exceptions, after 1964 the composition of our coinage changed to a copper-nickel alloy. The nickel is found in the outside layers largely to retain a color similar to the previous silver issues. The layers of these coins become apparent when the coin is turned on edge.

Ninety percent gold and 10% copper is the most often found composition of most U.S. regular issue and commemorative gold coins.

The gold U.S. Eagle bullion coin is composed of 91.67% gold, 3% silver and 5.33% copper. The silver Eagle is 99.93% silver and .07% copper. Each of these coins, however, contains a full ounce of precious metal.

The composition and weight of U.S. coins was until the 1850s such that the actual metal content value was virtually identical to and sometimes even greater than the coin's face value.

The effect was to drive out of circulation what few minor coins there were that had not been melted and to give rise to a number of alternative units of exchange--tokens, fractional currency, and the foreign coins from many nations.

In 1853 the problem of a diminished supply of circulating coins was addressed by reducing the weight of the half dime, dime, quarter and half dollar. This weight reduction was evidenced by the addition of arrows at the date and/or rays on the reverse of coins dated 1853-1855.

After the mints had made concerted efforts to provide a large supply of minor coins for exchange purposes, the arrows and rays were removed. At about this time half cents and Large cents had finally reached the end of their usefulness. These coins had simply become too cumbersome and costly for continued use in general circulation. Consequently, the size of the cent was greatly reduced, and the copper in its composition has become less and less so that our most current cents are composed of only 2.5% of the metal.

As confidence was lost in paper currency with the impending Civil War, all types of coins began to quickly disappear from circulation. All manner of ingenious alternatives were substituted. Again tokens, fractional currency, even postage stamps were used in everyday transactions.

By 1873, although fractional coins were now available for circulation, arrows next to the date again became necessary to indicate a slight rise in the weight of dimes, quarter dollars and half dollars.

Also at about this time a special silver dollar-sized coin known as a "Trade Dollar" was minted to compete with Mexican and other foreign dollar-sized coins in the Orient. To place this coin on a competitive footing, the weight (and thereby amount of silver) was raised about 2% above the standard silver dollar.

With many minor changes in weights and compositions for individual denominations in the intervening years, the final blow to intrinsic value was struck by the Coinage Act of 1965. This act called for the elimination or reduction of silver from the coins of general circulation and was made necessary by the upward pressure of the free market price of silver. Until the 1960s, the Treasury was willing to sell silver at $1.2929 an ounce. With the depletion of the Treasury's stockpile of silver dollars and bullion, however, by 1967 it became apparent that restrictions on such sales had become necessary. The refusal of the Treasury to continue sales combined with its prohibition on the melting of the hoards of coins withdrawn by the general public further escalated the price rises in the metal.

In a few short years, silver coins had completely disappeared from circulation and Gresham's Law had been obeyed. The government saw the futility of minting additional silver coins.

COIN DATING

Another readily noticeable feature of virtually every United States coin is the date of issue. Usually found on the obverse side of the coin, the date with some exceptions indicates the year in which the coin was minted. In some years, remarkably, no coins of some denominations were minted at all. In 1815, for example, no half cents, cents, half dimes or dimes were produced by the mint.

Especially in the early days of coinage it was not uncommon for dies to be re-engraved so that a later date is found engraved over an earlier one. This practice gave rise to many varieties of overdates. Dramatic examples of such superimpositions are found on the 1807 over 6 cent and even on the relatively recent 1942 over 1 dime. Much research had been conducted as to the circumstances that surrounded overdating techniques and decisions. Collectors have even been known to specialize in the uncovering of new varieties of this sort and to build collections with overdating as the focus.

In a particularly famous exception to dating coins in the year of mintage, silver dollars dated 1804 are generally believed to have been minted in the 1830s, mainly as souvenirs for presentation sets. This date also appears on a number of restrikes struck for collectors as late as 1859.

An even more common practice in the early days of the mint was to use dies until they were no longer serviceable without regard to the actual years in which the coins were being struck. Mintage figures by year for this period are notoriously unreliable.

In 1964 with the drain of silver coins from circulation and consequent shortage, the Treasury sought to respond by doubling the various mints' annual production of coins. Congress aided this effort by permitting the 1964 date on coins regardless of year minted. It was supposed that such high mintage figures would discourage any thought of these coins becoming collectors' items. Intrinsic value of course was soon to defeat this plan for coins struck in silver. However, the initial clad coins (dated 1965-1967) were often struck in a year later than the date found on the coin.

Another dimension of the date that is found on a coin can be seen in changes that have taken place in the size and style of numerals.

My own introduction to coin collecting was sparked by the 1960 "small date" craze. That year, two somewhat different sized numerals are found on the Lincoln cent. The smaller of the two dates, especially those from the Philadelphia mint, were initially seen as quite valuable and were much sought after. In retrospect the frenzy seems quite unwarranted. Examples of the "small date" minted in Denver can easily be had for 5-10 cents each. The scarcer one from Philadelphia sells for $2 and demand for it has all but vanished.

Our earliest coinage provides all sorts of varieties of date sizes and numeral styles of interest mainly to specialists.

This is not to say that such considerations as those above have no significant impact on coin prices and overall desirability. Undoubtedly, the 1960 small date cents were not as rare as originally thought. And the value of many "varieties" can be quite ephemeral. I can remember when the price difference between the small and large date variety of the 1857 Large cent was much more marked. Today the price gap seems to have all but closed.

The price of overdates and other varieties in the date on a coin is much more a function of rarity and popularity than of other components. Even then the scarcity of some items can long go unrecognized or become buried in an unpopular series. Most often relatively small differences in date design are completely ignored.

Much more will be said about pricing and value considerations in Chapter 5.

MINT MARKS

The mint mark is an important feature in the design of a coin because it shows which mint struck a particular coin and also is quite necessary in determining a coin's value. Since eight different mints have produced coins small letters are placed on a coin in various locations to indicate the mint of origin.

Philadelphia, Pa.	"P"	1793 to present
Charlotte, N.C.	"C"	1838-1861
Dahlonega, Ga.	"D"	1838-1861
New Orleans, La.	"O"	1838-1861, 1879-1909
San Francisco, Ca.	"S"	1854-1955, 1968 to present
Carson City, Nev.	"CC"	1870-1893
Denver, Colo.	"D"	1906 to present
West Point, N.Y.	"W"	1984 to present

The location of the mint mark can be either the obverse or reverse of a coin dated before 1968. Since 1968 all mint marks are found on the coin's obverse.

Until recently, with the exception of a few years of wartime nickel production (1942-1945), coins produced at the Philadelphia mint bear no mint mark.

The following rules of thumb will be helpful in determining the existence and/or location of a mint mark on each of the various denominations.

Half Cents—no mint mark (Philadelphia).

Cents (through 1907)—no mint mark (Philadelphia).

Indian Cents (1908 and 1909)—"S" mint mark on reverse, bottom center.

Lincoln Cents (1909 to present)—"S" or "D" mint marks on obverse below date.

Two-Cents—no mint mark (Philadelphia).

Nickel Three-Cents—no mint mark (Philadelphia).

Shield Nickels—no mint mark (Philadelphia).

Liberty Nickels (1912)—"D" or "S" on reverse lower left between "Cents" and "United."

Buffalo Nickel—"D" or "S" on reverse bottom center along rim.

Jefferson Nickel (1939-1964)—"D" or "S" on reverse right center along rim.

(1942-1945)—"P," "S," or "D," on reverse large letter above Monticello.

(1965-1967)—no mint mark (Philadelphia).

(1968 to date)—"P," "D," or "S," on obverse below date along rim.

Silver Three-Cents (In 1851)—"O" on reverse right center at the opening of the design.

Half Dimes (1838-1873)—"O" or "S" on reverse lower center within or outside wreath.

Early Dimes (to 1916)—"O," "CC," "S," or "D" as above on half dimes until Mercury type.

Mercury Dimes (1916-1945)—"D" or "S" on reverse lower left along rim between "One" and "Dime."

Roosevelt Dimes (1946-1964)—"D" or "S" on reverse lower left above "E" in "One."

(1965-1967)—no mint mark (Philadelphia).

(1968 to date)—"P," "D," or "S" on obverse above date.

Twenty Cents—"CC" on reverse below eagle.

Early Quarters (to 1916)—"O," "S," "CC," or "D" on reverse below eagle.

Standing Liberty Quarters (1916-1930)—"D" or "S" on obverse left of date.

Washington Quarters (1932-1964)—"D" or "S" on reverse below branch.

(1965-1967)—no mint mark (Philadelphia).

(1968 to date)—"P," "D," or "S" on obverse above date.

Early Halves (1838-1839)—"O" on obverse above date.

(1840-1915)—"O," "S," "CC," or "D" on reverse below eagle.

Walking Liberty Halves (1916)—"D" or "S" on obverse below "In God we Trust."

(1917)—as above and also on reverse along rim at 7 o'clock.

(1918-1947)—"D" or "S" on reverse as above.

Franklin Halves (1948-1963)—"D" or "S" on reverse under "States."

Kennedy Halves (1964)—"D" on reverse below eagle's left claw.

(1965-1967)—no mint mark (Philadelphia).

(1968 to date)—"P," "D," or "S" on obverse below neck of Kennedy.

Early Dollars (to 1873)—"O," "CC," or "S" on reverse below eagle.

Trade Dollars (1873-1855)—"CC" or "S" on reverse below eagle.

Morgan Dollars (1878-1921)—"O," "CC," "S," or "D" on reverse below wreath.

Peace Dollars (1921-1935)—"D" or "S" on reverse along rim under "One."

Eisenhower Dollars (1971-1978)—"D" or "S" on obverse below neck of Eisenhower.

Anthony Dollars (1979-1981)—"P," "D," or "S" on obverse on Anthony's right shoulder.

$1 Gold (1849-1870)—"C," "D," "O," or "S" on reverse under wreath.

$2.50 Gold (1839-1839)—"C," "D," or "O" on obverse above date.

(1840-1907)—"C," "D," "O," or "S" on reverse at bottom above "2½."

(1908-1929)—"D" on reverse lower left along rim.

$3 Gold (1854-1870)—"D" "O," or "S" on reverse below wreath.

$4 Gold—no mint mark (Pattern coins).

$5 Gold (Early issues to 1837)—no mint mark (Philadelphia).

(1838-1839)—"C" or "D" on obverse above date.

(1840-1907)—"C," "D," "O," "S," or "CC" on reverse at bottom above "Five."

(1908-1929)—"D," "S," or "O" on reverse lower left along rim.

$10 Gold (to 1907)—"O," "S," or "CC" on reverse above "Ten."

(1907-1933 (Indian))—"D" or "S" on reverse along rim at 7 o'clock.

$20 Gold (Liberty type to 1907)—"O," "S," or "CC" on reverse above "Twenty."

Saint-Gaudens Type (1907-1933)—"D" or "S" on obverse above near date.

Commemorative Coins—Various locations. Recent commemoratives have obverse mint marks.

Bullion Coins

$1 Silver Eagle (1986 to date)—"S" on reverse left of eagle's tail.

$25 ½ oz. Gold Eagle (1987 to date)—"W" on obverse within lower right rays.

$50 1 oz. Gold Eagle (1986 to date)—"W" on obverse within lower right rays.

Other denominations of bullion gold coins do not have mint marks.

OBVERSE AND REVERSE

The obverse, or front, of a coin is the side which presents the most important design features. Generally, a coin series will take on the name of this feature. (There are some exceptions, notably the "Buffalo" nickel.) Most often the obverse is comprised of a bust or head of a famous or fictional person. Heads of presidents, Indians and, of course, The Goddess of Liberty—sitting, standing, walking, head left and head right—have been most popular.

As mentioned before, the date is generally found on the obverse side of a coin.

The reverse or back side of a coin is defined as the side opposite the important design feature. The eagle, in any number of poses, has been selected most often to grace this side of our coinage. Fasces, wreaths, buildings and the Liberty Bell are distant seconds in this competition.

The denominations of most coins is found on the reverse, sometimes the mint mark, and assorted inscriptions and mottos.

A list of mottos, inscriptions and other miscellaneous design features are found below:

Mottos

E Pluribus Unum—Found on the reverse of early coins as part of the Great Seal. Literally, it means "From Many, One," and is undoubtedly a reference to the union of the original and subsequent states. This motto is now a standard feature of all current coins. Its history as a design feature has not been an uninterrupted one. For years it was found absent from our coinage.

In God We Trust—First appearing on two-cent coins in 1864, this motto now appears on all U.S. coins. Briefly, in 1907, there was a flap when through the efforts of President Theodore Roosevelt the motto was removed from the $10 and $20 gold coin as inconsistent with official church-state separation. As might have been expected, a huge public outcry ensued and the motto was restored in 1908.

Inscriptions

United States of America—Was to be placed on the reverse of all coins under the same law which established the Mint. On many commemorative coins this inscription is found on the obverse.

Liberty—To be placed on the obverse of all coins under the same law that established the Mint. Often found in Liberty's hair and, ironically, one of the first devices to wear away on a circulating coin.

Other Devices

Designer's Initials—Not found on U.S. coins until the 1849 $1 gold coin, the initials of the engraver are often quite inconspicuous and may appear on either the obverse or reverse of a coin. On our most recent coinage these initials can be found as follows:

Cent—V.D.B. (Victor D. Brenner)—on the obverse along the rim under Lincoln's shoulder.

Five-cent—F.S. (Felix Schlag)—now located on the obverse along the rim under Jefferson's shoulder.

Dime—J.S. (John Sinnock)—found on the obverse under the forward portion of Roosevelt's neck.

Quarter—J.F. (John Flanagan)—located on the obverse at the base of Washington's neck.

Half dollar—G.R. (Gilroy Roberts)—designed the obverse. His initials are found on the lower portion of the neck of Kennedy's bust.

—F.G. (Frank Gasparro)—designed the reverse. His initials are found on the reverse at the right of the eagle's tail.

Anthony dollar—F.G. (Frank Gasparro)—found on the reverse beneath the eagle.

Major Portraits, Places, and Symbols on U.S. Coinage

The Goddess Liberty—Appears throughout the history of U.S. coinage as a symbol of unextinguished freedom. She is dressed in a war bonnet on the obverse of the $10 gold piece beginning in 1907.

Six presidents—Lincoln (Cent), Jefferson (Five-Cent), Roosevelt (Dime), Washington (Quarter), Kennedy (Half Dollar), Eisenhower (Dollar).

Benjamin Franklin and Susan B. Anthony—With the exception of the presidents mentioned above, Franklin and Anthony are the only other actual persons to have found their way onto regularly issued coinage. Franklin, of course, holds a special place as a statesman and founder of our country.

Anthony was a prominent pioneer of women's rights. Heightened sensitivity to women's issues in the 1970s undoubtedly led to her appearance on the dollar coin. Regrettably, the coin has seen very little circulation.

Buildings—The Lincoln Memorial was placed on the reverse of the Lincoln cent beginning in 1959.

Jefferson's home, Monticello is found on the reverse of the five-cent piece.

The eagle—The national bird has been the most popular and recurring symbol found on the reverse of our coinage. (It also appears as an obverse device on the cents of 1856-1858 and the Gobrecht Dollar of 1836-1839.) Found even on the very recent bullion silver and gold coins, some particularly majestic examples grace later gold coins and silver dollars. However, the example found on early $5 gold pieces appears extremely scrawny and unattractive.

The shield—This device is often found on the reverse of our coinage, upon the eagle's breast, or on the obverse resting against the seated Liberty.

Arrows and olive branches—Usually found in the talons of the full-faced eagle, symbolizing at the same time a readiness for war and a hope for peace.

Indian princess—Found on the one-cent coin of 1859-1909 and the $1 gold coin from 1854 to 1889 among others, the model for these coins is reputed to have been the engravers daughter, Sarah Longacre.

The Indian chief—The obverse of the five-cent "Buffalo" nickel, as it is sometimes called, is actually a composite portrait of three Indian Chiefs (Iron Tail, Two Moons and John Tree). An unidentified chief sat for the $2.50 and $5 gold coins of 1908-1929.

The buffalo—"Black Diamond" was the model for the reverse of the five-cent piece of 1913-1938.

The wreath—Another very popular reverse, especially for our early coinage, the wreath is sometimes found alone as a device, as on the Large cent; at other times it appears with another symbol, as with the shield on the Indian cent of 1860-1909. The wreath most often appears to be composed of oak or laurel branches, but is identified as a composite of tobacco, cotton, wheat and corn on the Flying Eagle cent of 1856-1858.

Fasces—Found on the reverse of the Winged Liberty dime of 1916-1945, the fasces is a bundle of rods encasing an ax with its head protruding meant to symbolize officialdom.

Liberty Bell—Found as the prominent device on the reverse of the Franklin half dollars (1948-1963), and later superimposed upon the moon on the reverse of the Eisenhower dollar commemorating the Bicentennial.

Victory torch and branches—This design is presented on the reverse of the Roosevelt dime. The torch symbolizes liberty. The oak branch on the right and the olive branch on the left are to remind us of strength and peace respectively.

Presidential coat of arms—This symbol, which includes a number of those spoken about above, graces the reverse of the Kennedy half dollar (1964 to Present).

Misc. Symbols	Where Found	Symbolizes
Chain	Large Cents 1793 (Reverse)	Strength of Union of States (Links)
Wheat Ears	Lincoln Cents 1909-1958 (Reverse)	Prosperity
13 Rays	1866 Shield Nickel (Reverse)	13 Original States
13 Stars	Shield Nickels 1866-1883 (Reverse)	13 Original States
Sun	Saint-Gaudens $20 Gold 1907-1933 (Reverse)	Exact origin unclear
Six Pointed Star	Three-Cent Silver Coins 1851-1864 (Obverse)	Exact origin unclear
Five Pointed Star	$4 Gold (Reverse)	Exact origin unclear

Bicentennial Designs	Denomination
Colonial Drummer	Quarter
Independence Hall	Half Dollar
Liberty Bell and Moon	Dollar

COIN RELIEF AND HIGH POINTS

Coin relief refers to the relation the features of a coin have to the field. On virtually all U.S. coins minted over the years the design features are raised, sometimes called "bas-relief." They extend above the field and thereby these high points of the design show the most wear on a circulated coin.

An extreme example of bas-relief occurred on some 1907 $20 Saint-Gaudens gold coins. The relief was so pronounced that stacking the coins was impractical. A few proofs were minted as pattern pieces with an extremely high relief such that the coin has an almost concave appearance.

The Indian Head $2.50 and $5 gold coins are different from all other U.S. coins in just the opposite way that high relief coins are. They have a recessed or incused design. The design features are below the field.

When grading coins an absolute necessity is a familiarity with what portions or features of the design experience the inevitable wearing as the coin changes hands in circulation. Even slight wear on the very highest points of the design can make huge differences in grading and price. It is conceivable that simply sliding a high grade uncirculated coin across a table can subtract thousands of dollars from its value to a collector.

COIN EDGES AND MILLING

There is more to a coin than its obverse or reverse. What? Surprisingly, the edges of coins are vastly different. Currently, one-cent and five-cent pieces have plain edges. And generally minor coins, those composed of base metals, have been minted without the reeded edges found on the clad dimes, quarters and halves that circulate today.

Coins minted of precious metals have been known to encourage certain abuses. One obvious one involves scraping small quantities of the metal from the edge of a coin and then passing it along at full face value. The scrapings could then be sold.

To lessen the likelihood of this practice steps were taken to make tampering of this sort more difficult. Plain edges would not accomplish this. Consequently, U.S. silver and gold coins, almost from the beginning, were minted with small, vertical serrations on the edge, called "reeds."

Notable exceptions are found on 50-cent pieces where stars and lettering along with intermittent reeding can be found, depending on the date of the half dollar, up until 1836. Early silver dollars through 1803 also have lettered edges with decorations attesting to the denomination of the issue.

The very earliest half cents and Large cents have various designs and lettering on the edges. Ten-dollar gold pieces, minted from 1907-1933, can be found with the number of stars corresponding to the states in the Union at the time. The Saint-Gaudens $20 gold pieces of 1907 have the date inscribed on the rim as well as on the obverse. In fact, the rarer variety presents the date in Roman numerals.

One would expect that the reeding, especially on later coins, would be fairly uniform. A small number of studies have shown otherwise. Wide variances in the number of reeds have even been found on the Roosevelt dime, for example.

HOW A COIN IS MANUFACTURED

The process of minting coins is much like that of any firm that stamps or fashions small parts. The Mint must, of course, proceed with much greater care since its products are legal tender and since "rejects," if security is lax, may well enter the collector market as valuable mint errors.

Simply put, from mine to Federal Reserve Bank, a coin is made through an eight-step process.

1. A mining company extracts the ore (copper, nickel, silver, gold or iron) from the ground.

2. The metal is smelted or refined and the finished product in the form of coils of strip metal or planchets is shipped to the Mint.
3. The Mint cleans, weighs and then punches the metal into blanks which are slightly larger than the finished coin will be.
4. These blanks are annealed, which is a heating process used to make the metal more receptive to striking and thereby cause less wear and tear on the dies.
5. These blanks then go through a process called "upsetting" which provides the coin with a raised rim. This allows for a more uniform feeding and striking process.
6. These planchets are fed into a coin press where both the obverse and reverse of the coin are struck from dies. These dies are the products of the original design for the coin and are fashioned in a lengthy process from models to master dies.

   At the same time the coin is being struck by the obverse and reverse dies, a collar, in effect an "edge die," fashions a smooth or reeded edge on the coin depending on the denomination being struck.
7. The finished products are inspected. All coins must meet specifications with regard to weight, size and fineness. Coins not within certain tolerance limits or coins which are defective in some way due to misstriking are rejected.
8. Finally, acceptable coins are counted and bagged for ultimate shipment to your pocket or purse through the banking system.

A NOTE ON MINTAGE FIGURES

As you can imagine coins cost the government less to make then their actual value as legal tender. This is especially true now that precious metals have all but disappeared from U.S. coins. The difference in the cost of production and face value of coins is called "seigniorage." It represents the profit the government makes by minting coins.

Sometimes, as has happened several times in the history of U.S. coinage, the intrinsic value or metal worth of coins increases to a level at or above the coin's face value. When this happens the coins quickly disappear from circulation.

Most recently this happened with all our 90% and 40% silver coins. Close calls have come even with pennies of late. The price of copper per pound has nearly crept over the point where melting cents would be marginally profitable.

How many coins are minted in a year?

Recently released figures (*Coin World*, Feb. 17, 1988) from the Mint give the following totals by denomination for 1987:

Cents	9,564,317,305
Nickels	784,550,945
Dimes	1,418,373,743
Quarters	1,240,555,037
Halves	1,434,541

This total of around 13 billion coins compares with about 12 billion produced in 1986, 3.3 billion in 1961, and roughly 1.4 billion in 1951.

Since the very beginning of official coinage in the U.S., the Mint has produced:

	Pieces	Dollar Total
Gold Coins*	351,545,358	4,526,218,477.50
Silver Coins*	17,123,584,252	3,877,054,052.10
Clad Coins	26,543,787,055	5,929,542,320.00
Minor Coins	143,359,781,381	2,116,186,993.00
	187,378,698,046	16,449,001,842.60

*Not including recent commemoratives and bullion coins.

Estimates have been given that as many as $1/3$ of all gold coins minted were melted into bars in 1933-1934. No reliable estimates have ever been produced for the "great silver melt" that began in the middle 1960s and may well continue today since the silver value of many coins is well above their numismatic and face value.

But putting aside any adjustments for the melting of coins which has happened officially and unofficially throughout the history of U.S. coinage, we might still venture estimates for how many coins have been minted per capita.

If we divide the population of the U.S. into a rough estimate of the number of coins "out there," we may be astounded to realize that the mint has produced about 750 coins ($64 in coin) for each of us. In fact, each of us should have about 500 cents somewhere in our possession. In 1987 alone, the Mint arranged to supply everyone in the U.S. with 38 pennies. Where have they all gone?

When we realize that 30 years ago we were getting along with cent productions of one-tenth those of today, and that the production itself accumulates, the need for current production levels seems incredible.

One way to account for part of the drain of cents from circulation can be found when we realize that all Lincoln cents through 1958 (the wheat cents) have a slight numismatic value and therefore no longer circulate.

Even then, 126 billion cents have been produced. Are significant numbers lost? Or saved in drawers and piggy banks and seen as not worth carrying around? No one seems to know. As a personal reckoning you might try to count all the pennies you have around the house. Are you above or below the per capita penny wealth level of the U.S.?

MINT ERRORS

With all the billions of coins produced at the Mint, a few substandard coins escape the inspection process. Sometimes these defective coins are the result of dramatic errors in the production process. Most often they are due to very minor variations in die or striking conditions.

Essentially, there are three types of errors that may occur in the minting process. Coins of course, may be altered or damaged outside the mint; however, we will reserve the term "error" for governmental alteration or damage.

Planchet and Blanking Errors

This sort of error is usually due to a defect in the "raw material" of the minting process. The planchet may be either overweight or underweight, or be the wrong metal for the denomination being struck. With the current clad coinage the planchet may more readily split or flake. Such errors occurred much less frequently with earlier coinage.

Striking Errors

Coins can be struck off-center when the planchet is not completely lined up with the die.

Double strikes occur when a coin is not expelled from the collar after the initial striking. Should a coin remain stuck in the die, it will produce an incused design on subsequent planchets that are fed into the press. These are called "capped die strikes."

Another type of doubling can happen if various parts of the production machinery are not tightly fitted so that a "bouncing" of the coin takes place giving the design a blurred appearance in whole or in part.

If two coins enter the collar at the same time, each will be struck on just one side. The remaining side will be blank.

Weak strikes are the result of worn dies or at the end of a striking run when lower coining pressures occur as a result of the presses being turned off.

Die Errors

Due to the extreme pressure needed for the coining process, the coin die experiences a great deal of stress. These stresses result in damage to the die in the form of cracks, chips and scratches. Such damage to the dies is evident on a coin since metal from the planchet will, under pressure, fill any indentations on the die, thus leaving a raised area on the coin.

A "cud" is a die broken to such an extent that a piece of the die actually breaks off. As the planchet is struck metal flows into the empty area and appears as a blob of metal on the resulting coin.

The opposite problem occurs when portions of the die are filled with debris. On coins struck under these circumstances areas of the design will be missing or weak.

When care is not taken in the alignment of the dies, the obverse and reverse side of a coin can be rotated outside the normal 180 degrees alignment called for by mint specifications. This is called a rotated die error.

Changes made to existing dies, while not errors as such, result in coin oddities. Engraved over-dates and mint marks are the most common design feature changes that are made on existing dies, although lettering and portrait changes occur often also.

Most mint errors are surprisingly inexpensive. The existing supply of dramatic errors is quite small. But demand is not great either.

From our proceeding discussion I have listed major types of errors with a range of prices dependent mainly on the denomination and age of the series. Older coins and higher denomination coins are generally more expensive. Prices listed are for coins that otherwise might grade XF or better.

Quarter Dollar Struck on a Dime Planchet

Improper Planchet—$25 to $2,000.
Probably the most expensive error. Especially valuable on obsolete and recent $1 coins.
Split Planchet or Lamination Errors—$1 to $50.
Splitting of planchet must be considerable.
Incomplete Planchet—$1 to $100.
Again, missing portion must be considerable.

Large Cent Struck 50% Off-Center

Off-Center Strike—$1 to $1,000.

Very dependent on percentage of design missing; 25-50% is the minimum requirement for the value of the error to be significant.

Double Struck Liberty Capped Large Cent

Double Strike—$10 to $500.

Additional strikes add to the value of the error.

1979 Lincoln Capped Die Strike

Capped Die Strikes—$25 to $200.

Image of other strikes is clear on most valuable specimens of this error.

One-Sided Strike—$10 to $500.

Blank Planchet—$1 to $200.

Weak Strikes—Usually **decreases** the value of the coin.

Cuds and Die Breaks—$5 to $250.

Filled Die—$1 to $25.

Certain exceptions exist, for example the 1922 cent, where the mint mark was filled. When errors become recognized and catalogued their prices increase considerably.

Rotated Dies—$1 to $25.

Re-engravings—Very dependent on date and recognition accorded to the re-engraving.

5

Determining a Coin's Value

What's it worth? The question seems simple enough but the answer is not. For, in a sense, coins have many values. Let us first look at a few of the different ways the question of worth can be answered, and then turn to the factors that, taken together, determine value.

Catalogue value—This is the price listed in a book like this one. It is an attempt to set out the average price for which a coin retails and is arrived at by comparing the prices at which many sellers are willing to part with a particular coin. It is not, however, an offering price since the author of the catalogue may not even be a dealer and, consequently, have no coins for sale. Further, since catalogues are printed far less frequently than a dealer's price list, it is often the case that a catalogue price can become quite dated. Also, it is not unusual for a dealer to offer coins at a percentage of catalogue price. You can see then how unrealistic it would be to think that the price you have found in the catalogue is the one you will eventually or easily receive for your coin. Better to think of this price as a "ballpark" figure from which a deal can be struck.

Retail value—This is the price at which a dealer may offer a coin. There may be considerable variance in this price from dealer to dealer. Such a price is dependent on many factors including how much was paid for the coin, when it was purchased, how many of the particular item the dealer may possess, how many coins are being purchased in the deal, how large the overall transaction is, how hard the buyer is willing to bargain to acquire the coin, etc. Further, this is the value that will probably be placed on your coins if you ask for an appraisal or ask to have your collection valued for insurance purposes. Retail price is the closest to the replacement value of a coin.

35

Wholesale value—This is the price at which a dealer would expect to purchase a coin from a fellow dealer. The term is also used at times to indicate a quantity price at which a seller or buyer may be willing to exchange a large number of a particular item. Should a dealer make an offer on a coin or collection, it only makes sense that the offer will be somewhat below what he knows he would have to pay a supplier or wholesaler. The reason for this has to do with the fact that when the offer is made to the dealer, it is unlikely that this one coin will be something for which he has an immediate need. Also in buying a collection there will always be particular pieces that the dealer has little interest in buying. His lack of interest will be reflected in the offer he makes.

Buy Price—This is the price that a dealer is most likely to quote you when you persist in asking what your coin or collection is worth. You can see by now that this price will be substantially below what the dealer believes he can ask as a retail price. Most coins will have a buy price of something on the order of 50-75% of the price at which a dealer would retail the coin. If a coin is especially desirable, the offer may be as high as 90% of retail. Many coin publications have a section of want ads, where dealers nationwide place offers for coins that they especially need. Once you are able to properly identify the coins you have, these ads will give you a good idea of what you can expect to receive for them should you wish to sell.

FACTORS DETERMINING VALUE

Essentially, there are four factors that influence or determine the market price of a coin.

MINTAGE

A common mistake made by the novice collector is to think that "old" means "rare" and, therefore, "valuable." Actually, this is a confusion of categories. Older coins generally have lower mintages, but it is really the number of coins of an issue that were minted (or currently survive, which is also a function of age) that determines a coin's value.

Many Large cents of the early 1800s can be purchased for $5 to $10. Their mintages often run from 6-10 million. The 1857 issue, the last one, has a very low mintage at only one-third of a million. Though a later date, it is considerably more scarce than many earlier dates and commands a retail price of $30 or so in very good condition.

A small number of fairly recent coins are quite valuable because of low mintages. The 1931S Lincoln cent, the 1950D Jefferson nickel, and the 1931D and S Washington quarters are all keys to their series.

Simply by consulting mintage figures one could probably get a fairly good idea as to whether a coin is valuable. There is a confounding variable, however. The surviving number of some issues is considerably less than the quantity originally minted. This is because of melting, loss, or destruction of some other sort. For instance, the mintage of the 1903O Morgan dollar is quite high at 4.5 million. A fine specimen can retail for $150—10 to 15 times the price of silver dollars of far less mintage. Speculation has it that a large portion of this issue was melted under the Pittman Act of 1918. An exact figure on the number of extant 1903O dollars is, of course, not known. But if price is any indication, the number of coins of this issue that survive must be something well below a half million.

During the time around 1980, when silver soared to as high as $50 an ounce, many of the most recent silver coins were sent to the smelters. There have been any number of attempts by those who were buying large quantities of silver coins at that time to give, on the basis of their own sample, an estimate of how the melt might have gone on a date by date basis. It could well turn out that many coins thought to be very common are not so. It is doubtful that any rarities were created, but the unreliability of the mintage figures is nevertheless intriguing.

CONDITION

If the secrets to real estate value are location, location, and location, then the most overlooked factors in coin value are condition, condition, and condition. How well preserved a coin is, how close to its original mint state, how well it was struck, all these greatly affect the value of a coin. For example, a 1921S Walking Liberty half dollar can easily be purchased for $12 in good to very good condition. In mint state 65 (MS-65) you may well have to pay $25,000 for it. So few have survived in such pristine condition that a truly superb specimen can command such a large sum.

To complicate matters, it is difficult, if not impossible for the novice collector to tell the difference between a "super coin" such as the one described above and an MS-60 specimen (the lowest uncirculated grade) which sells for something on the order of $5,000.

Grading differences are found among circulated coins also, although here the price differences are moderate. This entire discussion is meant to drive home the point about how critical it is for the collector to gain experience in learning how to grade coins. This volume can only serve as an introduction to this art/science. Before you purchase or sell your first coin, you should obtain a good book on grading, preferably one with extensive drawings or photos. (See Chapter 16.)

The next step is to seek out someone who is knowledgeable about coins, preferably someone who does not desire to buy your coins or sell any to you. A coin club is usually a good place to find such a person. Ask to be shown a coin of the same series in each of the grades that are listed below. Nothing can take the place of this hands-on experience. The point here is to determine what passes for extremely fine condition when a disinterested party grades a coin *before* you realize the coin you bought actually grades far less. Especially at first, my advice would be to go very slowly, ask a lot of questions, compare the judgments of several people, and then take the plunge with low-priced coins where a mistake will not mean a severe monetary loss.

Grading is a very controversial area. Legitimate differences about how well preserved or worn a coin is can occur. And grading standards have shifted over the years even within the most prestigious grading bodies. The American Numismatic Association Certification Service is far stricter now than it was just a few years ago. Why this happened is anybody's guess, but I believe in part it was due to more educated buyers entering what had become a buyer's market. The tendency is always there to push the coins one has for sale a grade or two higher. After all, everyone wants to realize the best price they can get. Likewise, when buying, it is not uncommon to talk the coin down. These are some of the things that we come to expect in many of life's transactions. However, once these tendencies are recognized, your strategy should be not to buy or sell unless you and the other person can pretty much agree on the coin's grade. And this means you must do some homework. You must seek to close the advantage in grading knowledge that the other party in the transaction may have.

What follows are generic descriptions of the condition of U.S. coins. Each coin series or type has certain peculiarities regarding high points, etc., by which wear can be detected and calculated.

Fair/Poor (FA) Most of the design and date of the coin will be obliterated by extreme wear.

About Good (AG) Rims will be worn into the field of the coin. The date and the design will be partly worn away.

Good (G) Rims are fully distinct from the field. All of the large design features and dates are intact.

Very Good (VG) Rims, date and large design features are strong.

Fine (F) Medium-sized design features specific to the design are clear and distinct. All letters in "Liberty" show on appropriate coins.

Very Fine (VF) Slight wear apparent on the highest features. All lettering is sharp.

Extremely Fine (XF) Large and medium design features are sharp. Some mint luster remains.

Almost Uncirculated (AU) All original design features are sharp. Only slight wear or light rubbing is visible on the highest features. Mint luster is almost completely intact.

Uncirculated (UNC) or (MS-60) No wear or rubbing can be found on the most prominent design features. Luster is intact, although there may be small marks and scratches evident in the field of the coin.

Choice Uncirculated (CU) or (MS-65) A well struck uncirculated coin. Bag marks and other abrasions are minimal. Full mint luster has been retained.

  * *Proof* (PR) A description often included in the grading of coins. However, this description better refers to a special striking process in which care has been taken to bring about an especially well-struck coin, not permitted to come into contact with other coins, and consequently free of all marks and abrasions. Such a coin, of course, can have been mishandled at the mint or afterward. Some have even been known to circulate. Consequently, there can be different grades of proof coins.

The photos below show the Walking Liberty half dollar in each of the grades from about good to uncirculated.

About Good

Good

Very Good

Fine

Very Fine

Extremely Fine

Almost Uncirculated

Uncirculated

When assessing the condition of a coin there are other important aspects beyond the wear that the coin may have undergone. Below is a handy check list. Listed first are things that detract from a coin's appearance and value:

_____Cleaned. It is almost never the case that the normal cleaning agents for copper, nickel, silver or gold can be used on coins. If a coin looks cleaned its worth is less. Copper cleaner, for instance, gives copper coins a shiny appearance, but since it is an abrasive, the coin's surface suffers greatly. A silver coin when dipped in silver cleaners takes on an unnatural appearance that no experienced collector would mistake for luster. Once a coin is pitted or dark there is not much that can be done about it. Cleaning will only make things worse. Most coins must be dropped a grade or two if cleaning has taken place. It is almost always a good idea to avoid purchasing such coins. Wait for one with no problems to come along. In the long run, it will be much easier to sell.

_____Scratches, rim nicks, abrasions, dents. All seriously affect a coin's value.

_____Weak strike. When a great many coins are struck from the same die, the clarity of the impression gradually lessens. Even an uncirculated coin make lack certain high relief features because of this. In extreme cases large elements of the design may be very unclear.

_____Spots, discolorations, carbon spots. Copper coins especially suffer from exposure to the elements. Corrosion and pitting must be looked for on early copper coins. And, strange as it seems, even very recent coins can be affected. Proof sets, sealed in their original government packaging sometimes develop white spots on the silver coins and carbon spots on the cent.

_____Holes. When coins have been used as jewelry often a hole has been drilled in them so that they can be worn on a chain. To disguise this the hole may be filled. However, in every case, the the value of the coin is greatly affected.

The absence of all of the above defects combined with some or all of the features listed below usually enhance a coin's value:

_____Strong strike. Early strikes from a die show more of the detail of the design. Coins with evidence of a full strike are much sought after and command considerable premiums. Full steps on the reverse of the Jefferson nickel, a full split band on the reverse of the Mercury dime, a full head on the obverse of the Standing Liberty quarter dollar, full bell lines on the reverse of the Franklin half dollar are all evidence of strong strikes.

_____Toning. A very small number of mostly uncirculated coins react to the elements such that the surface of the coin takes on a mellow, even quality that at times can even be iridescent. Where the toning is uneven the eye appeal and thereby value of the coin is lessened.

POPULARITY

In 1960, when I first began to collect coins, Lincoln pennies were the rage. Everyone, it seemed, wanted to fill the penny boards that provided a hole for each date and mint mark. Since then not only has the lowly Lincoln fallen from favor, but date collecting itself has given way to other styles of collecting. Today silver dollars, gold, and type coins are quite popular. Silver dollars never seem to lose favor with the collecting public. Especially in the uncirculated grades, a silver dollar will often sell for much more than a coin from another series that is of a comparable grade and mintage. For example, one can only imagine how much an 1871 silver three-cent piece would command if the series were as popular as Morgan dollars. The mintage of this coin was only 4,360 and yet it retails for around $650 in the lowest uncirculated grade. Hardly anyone collects this series by date and so the demand for a coin of any particular year is very low. Typically, a collector would want such a coin only as an instance of the type it represents.

Fads come and go in coin collecting as in everything else. Sometimes it pays to stay off the beaten path and simply collect what interests you. Who knows, maybe popularity will eventually coincide with your interests and you will be on the ground floor price-wise.

METAL CONTENT

Every U.S. silver and gold coin has what can be called a "floor" value or "junk" value based on its metal content. Presumably, a coin cannot be worth less than this unless part of it is missing or the coin is so worn that its metal content (by weight or fineness) is not clear. Or, as we shall see directly, the transaction involving it is so inconsequential as not to be worth the time of the buyer.

On the other hand, many silver coins have no significant value over the silver content. Consequently, the junk value and the price at which one would realistically expect to sell that same coin to a dealer (its numismatic value) are the same.

Let us take some examples which will permit us to elaborate on the chart that follows.

Case #1. We find a badly worn 1934 Walking Liberty half dollar. It is discolored and has some small dents in the rim. In this condition common silver coins have no numismatic value. However, if the spot price of silver for today is $8.00/oz., we can calculate the silver value of the half dollar by multiplying the weight of the coin, 192.9 grains (about .4 oz. since there are 480 grains per ounce) times the fineness (the metal content of the coin is 90% silver) times the going price of silver.

$$.402 \text{ oz.} \times .90 \times \$8 = \$2.89$$

So that ugly half dollar is worth roughly six times its face value. Why roughly? Well, we should not lose sight of the fact that this is only one coin. Could we fault a dealer who offered us only $2.50 or even $2.00 for the coin? I think not. After all, we are still talking about less than a $1 profit for the dealer. Is such a transaction really worth his time? Should we have $100 face of comparable silver coins, it becomes more realistic to expect something very close to $578—the value of the silver alone in such coins.

Actually, in bag ($1,000 face) quantities, silver coins usually carry a small premium over the silver content. The premium probably derives from the ease with which the bags can be traded, the magic of owning silver pieces that were officially minted and actually circulated, or some such thing. However, there are times when this premium has disappeared and, in fact, as strange as it may sound, there are times when it is very difficult to obtain the full silver-content price for silver coins. Let me explain.

The price for silver coin bags might be called somewhat "inelastic" especially when the price of silver rises or falls dramatically. During the phenomenal run-up of the price of silver in 1980, when it peaked at around $50/oz., dealers were quite unwilling to pay much more than 20 to 25 times face. (If we use our chart we can see that even at $40/oz. silver coins should have commanded something like 28 times face—about $14 for a half dollar.)

Dealers claimed they were having difficulty receiving payments on a timely basis from smelters. And, when you think about it, this makes sense. At the time everybody was trying to have their coins melted into bars or other fabricated products, the smelters became backlogged and were unwilling to take the risk that prices would remain high. Dealers likewise began to lay off some of the risk through the lower prices they were willing to pay.

Quick price rises (and in some cases declines) are not necessarily going to be reflected immediately in the coin bag quotes you will receive. When the volatility ends, the bag price once again comes into line. A dealer, especially a small one, is naturally going to minimize his exposure to risk. If one wants better elasticity in price, then one might better hold silver bars, or silver stocks.

One easy way to keep abreast of "junk" silver coin bag prices is to consult *The Wall Street Journal*. On the commodities page, at the bottom of the column titled "Cash Prices," can be found a listing for "Coins, wholesale, $1,000 face value." Most large dealers would normally be willing to sell at this price and buy at from $200 to $500 less. Bag prices quoted in coin newspaper and magazine dealer ads will typically be several weeks or more out of date. The price in any actual transaction will almost always have to be negotiated by phone or in person that very day. Prices change hourly. So if you have an investment in this area, it is of paramount importance to find some way to keep current on prices.

Also, trading in smaller than bag quantities will mean a wider buy/sell price spread. Increasingly, dealers have sought to make distinctions in types of "junk" silver coins. As you might imagine, a bag of very worn silver coins will contain less silver than a bag containing coins that have seen little circulation. A spot check might be necessary to uncover this. Recently, half dollars, and coins from the earlier series (Mercury dimes and Walking Liberty halves) have become more desirable and command a slight additional premium of about $100 to $150 per bag. Common uncirculated silver coins are traded at a premium of from 5-10% over regular bag prices.

Case #2. Aunt Marcella has given you a 1921 silver dollar. The date is the year of her birth and she has had it a very long time. You don't wish to sell the coin but you do want to know its value so as to make a decision concerning how best to care for it.

The first thing you must do is correctly identify the piece. There were two types of silver dollars issued in 1921. The Peace type, in almost any condition has a numismatic value beyond its silver content. More likely, however, the dollar is of the Morgan type. In this case, unless the coin is in one of the highest grades, its value will be determined largely by the going price of silver. Dollars, because of their extreme popularity, have carried a significant premium above silver content making their price even more inelastic than other silver coins. Dollar bags, for which the 1921 Morgan is a staple, are quoted on the basis of 1,000 piece lots. With silver at $8/oz., bags trade in the $9,000-$10,000 area. The silver-content value for the bag would be something on the order of $6,200—making dollars a somewhat unsuitable way to invest in silver.

As you can see, Aunt Marcella's coin demands no special precautions be taken for its care. You could expect to receive something around $8 for it from a dealer, although I am sure your aunt will never forgive you should she learn of your sale. In fact, *most* people have trouble understanding how a piece they have prized for a lifetime commands such a paltry sum. You could easily buy one like it for around $11, however.

Case #3. A small coin accumulation, assembled by your grandfather, has been given to you upon his death. Included are three rolls of Kennedy half dollars. They do not look to be silver coins so you decide to spend them. But wait! Even though other denominations ceased being regularly issued in silver after 1964, half dollars were minted for general circulation with a 40% silver content from 1965-70. This part of your inheritance can be calculated as follows:

Weight		Silver Content		Spot Price		Value
.37 oz.	×	.40 fine	×	$8/oz.	=	$1.18

Your rolls ($10 face each) are worth about $23.60 each. Putting them in with your pocket change would certainly have been foolish.

Case #4. One other coin is often traded on the basis of its "junk" silver value. From 1942-45, due to a projected wartime shortage of nickel, the composition of the five-cent piece was changed to include 35% silver. Circulated pieces are identifiable by their darker gray color and the change in the placement and size of the mint mark. Both types of five-cent pieces were minted in 1942. So not every coin with that date will have silver value. In high grades these "silver nickels" have a numismatic value beyond the silver value. The value of low grade coins can be computed:

Weight		Silver Content		Spot Price		Value
.16 oz.	×	.35 Fine	×	$8/oz.	=	$.45

Quantities of less than a roll are of little interest to a dealer. With silver at $8/oz. expect to sell at about $18/roll and buy $22+/roll.

Case #5. While remodeling your house, you find a $5 Indian gold piece behind the woodwork. The rim has a number of large dents and the coin has been defaced from what appears to be a number of deep scratches. Should you be tickled with your find?

Well, gold coins, too, have a "junk" value. However, unlike silver coins, very few gold coins fall into this category. A gold coin must either be damaged or very severely worn not to have some numismatic value. Even then, such coins are good candidates for use in jewelry. The purchaser of a ring or pendant is usually not as concerned about a coin's condition since often only one side will show or the rim can be obscured by the setting.

Consequently, the floor price, calculated below and on our chart, represents the absolute lowest price an identifiable, complete $5 gold coin can be worth. Your baseboard find is a good one!

Weight		Gold Content		Spot Price		Value
.269 oz.	×	.90 Fine	×	$450/oz.	=	$108.84

*All the above calculations have been based on:
480 grains/troy oz.   1 gram = .0322 troy oz.
31.104 grams/troy oz.   1 gram = 15.4342 grains

Bullion Value of Silver Coins
(Per $1.00 Face Value)

Spot Price	Low Grade/ Circulated 10¢, 25¢, 50¢	40% Silver 50¢	Low Grade/ Circulated Silver War 5¢	Low Grade/ Damaged Silver $1.00
$5.00	$3.60	$1.48	$5.60	$3.87
$6.00	4.40	1.78	6.80	4.64
$7.00	5.10	2.08	8.00	5.42
$8.00	5.80	2.38	9.00	6.19
$9.00	6.50	2.66	10.00	6.96
$10.00	7.20	2.96	11.20	7.73
$11.00	8.00	3.26	12.40	8.51
$12.00	8.70	3.56	13.60	9.28
$13.00	9.40	3.86	14.70	10.05
$14.00	10.10	4.16	15.80	10.80
$15.00	10.90	4.46	17.00	11.60
$20.00	14.40	5.92	22.40	15.48
$30.00	21.60	8.88	33.60	23.19
$40.00	28.80	11.84	44.80	30.96
$50.00	36.00	14.80	56.00	38.69

Bag Quantities
(Wholesale price includes usual premium)

Spot Price	Low Grade/ Circulated 10¢, 25¢, 50¢ ($1000 Face)	40% Silver 50¢ ($1000 Face)	Unc. Common 10¢, 25¢, 50¢ ($1000 Face)	Common, Middle Grade Silver Dollars ($1000 Face)
$5.00	$3700-$4000	$1500-$1600	$3800-$4200	$6500-$7000
$6.00	4500- 4800	1800- 2000	4700- 5200	7500- 7900
$7.00	5200- 5500	2100- 2300	5500- 6000	8000- 8400
$8.00	6000- 6300	2400- 2600	6300- 6800	8500- 9000
$9.00	6800- 7100	2700- 2900	7000- 7400	9000- 9500
$10.00	7500- 7800	3000- 3200	7700- 8100	9500-10000
$11.00	8200- 8500	3300- 3500	8400- 8800	10000-10500
$12.00	8900- 9200	3600- 3800	9100- 9500	10500-11000
$13.00	9700-10000	3900- 4100	9900-10300	11000-11500
$14.00	10400-10700	4200- 4400	10600-11000	11500-12000
$15.00	11200-11500	4500- 4700	11400-11800	12000-12500

Bullion Value of Gold Coins
(Assumes the coin is damaged or otherwise uncollectable.)

Denomination

Spot Price	$1.00	$2.50	$5.00	$10.00	$20.00
$250.00	$12.10	$30.25	$60.50	$121.00	$242.00
$300.00	14.50	36.25	72.50	145.00	290.00
$350.00	17.00	42.50	85.00	170.00	339.00
$400.00	19.35	48.00	96.25	193.50	387.00
$450.00	21.80	54.50	109.00	218.00	435.00
$500.00	24.20	60.50	121.00	242.00	484.00
$550.00	26.60	66.50	133.00	266.00	532.00
$600.00	29.00	72.50	145.00	290.00	580.00
$700.00	33.80	84.50	169.00	338.00	676.00
$800.00	38.60	96.50	193.00	386.00	772.00
$900.00	43.40	108.50	217.00	434.00	868.00

VALUE AS A FUNCTION OF TIME AND KNOWLEDGE

Some, I suppose, would argue that in many cases a coin's value is a function of work (time) and knowledge. There is some truth to this—a truth that is often lost on a novice buyer or seller. Let me explain.

With regard to many inexpensive coins, the cost of the time and work involved in identifying, pricing, packaging, marketing, etc., often exceed any intrinsic worth that the coin may have. When one purchases a coin for $2 it may well be that the entire value of the coin can be written off to the costs of selling it. The real value of the coin consequently is derived from getting it to a point where a sale can be made. To speak in terms of resale then is to miss the point. How much is a roll of AU 1950D cents worth beyond its face value? Would it be out of the question for a dealer to charge 25 cents each for such a coin? And what portion of that price might one expect to recover upon a resale? Twenty-five cents does not represent the value of the coin in any sense other than the cost of selling it. One should expect to recover almost nothing with any attempt at resale.

Secondly, and somewhat more controversial, is the part that knowledge should play in the determination of worth. If I were to spend considerable time researching the relative scarcity of various types of early Large cents, am I obligated to make that knowledge available to ɑl who request an offer for their collection? Is my knowledge worth something? And is the value of that scarce variety I discover a product of my recognizing it as such?

These questions may well border on the area of business ethics; and therefore may well be outside the scope of this volume. But that is not to say that they will have no bearing on an actual transaction. Rather, I think, the average dealer expects to be compensated for his knowledge and experience. *How* that is to be done often remains fairly unclear to the party in the transaction who lacks the knowledge.

6
U.S. Minor Coinage

This chapter attempts to assess the value of U.S. coins composed of base metals, as opposed to precious metals, with the exception of our recent clad coinage which is discussed in Chapter 7 along with the silver coinage these clad coins were meant to replace.

VALUES OF MINOR COINS

Half Cents   Minted 1793/1857

Flowing Hair Type   Liberty Cap Type

Draped Bust Type

Classic Head Type   Braided Hair Type

Common Types		AG	G	GRADES F	XF	MS60
1793	Flowing Hair	500.00	1000.00	2100.00	6000.00	—
1794-7	Liberty Cap	60.00	150.00	400.00	1600.00	5000.00
1800-08	Draped Bust	8.00	20.00	40.00	150.00	650.00
1809-36	Classic Head	6.00	17.00	25.00	50.00	250.00
1840-57	Braided Hair	10.00	20.00	28.00	45.00	200.00

Many dates are considerably more expensive, notably:

	AG	G	GRADES F	XF	MS60
1794	80.00	250.00	500.00	2200.00	—
1795	80.00	200.00	450.00	2000.00	—
1796	1100.00	2200.00	6500.00	—	—
1797	100.00	300.00	550.00	2100.00	—
1802	150.00	350.00	1100.00	—	—
1811	50.00	100.00	300.00	1600.00	—

Some dates exist in proof only and are priced in the $3,000 to $4,000 range Proof-63.

Rare and expensive varieties are found on many dates.

Cents   Minted 1793-Date

Large Cents   Minted 1793/1857

Flowing Hair Type
(Chain Reverse)

Flowing Hair Type
(Wreath Reverse)

Liberty Cap Type

Draped Bust Type

Classic Head Type

Coronet Type
(Matron Head)

Coronet Type
(Mature Head)

		GRADES				
Common Types		AG	G	F	XF	MS60
1793	Flowing Hair					
	(Chain Reverse)	800.00	1600.00	3500.00	11,500.00	—
1793	Flowing Hair					
	(Wreath Reverse)	350.00	650.00	1500.00	6000.00	—
1794-1796	Liberty Cap	650.00	1400.00	3000.00	15,000.00	—
1796-1807	Draped Bust	10.00	20.00	60.00	400.00	2000.00
1808-1814	Classic Head	10.00	20.00	60.00	600.00	2200.00
1816-1857	Coronet Type	2.00	5.00	7.00	40.00	220.00

More expensive dates include:

			GRADES		
	AG	G	F	XF	MS60
1794	60.00	150.00	350.00	2000.00	—
1795	50.00	110.00	300.00	1750.00	—
1796	50.00	110.00	325.00	1750.00	—
1797	25.00	40.00	130.00	900.00	—
1798	15.00	35.00	125.00	900.00	—
1799	400.00	900.00	2800.00	—	—
1800	15.00	30.00	100.00	600.00	—
1801	15.00	25.00	100.00	600.00	—
1802	15.00	25.00	80.00	550.00	—
1803	10.00	20.00	80.00	550.00	—
1804	250.00	450.00	1400.00	6000.00	—
1805	15.00	25.00	80.00	550.00	—
1806	20.00	40.00	75.00	550.00	—
1807	10.00	22.00	80.00	550.00	—
1808	15.00	30.00	90.00	650.00	—
1809	30.00	65.00	325.00	1600.00	—
1810	15.00	25.00	90.00	600.00	—
1811	30.00	60.00	200.00	1000.00	—
1812	10.00	25.00	75.00	550.00	—
1813	15.00	30.00	125.00	700.00	—
1814	15.00	30.00	100.00	600.00	—
1821	5.00	10.00	45.00	450.00	1500.00
1823	20.00	35.00	170.00	1100.00	—
1857	10.00	25.00	35.00	85.00	250.00

Most dates have rare and/or more expensive varieties.

Prices for high grade circulated and uncirculated coins vary considerably due to factors such as overall eye appeal, mint luster, toning, etc.

Flying Eagle Cent   Minted 1857-58

	AG	G	GRADES F	XF	MS60
Common Type	4.00	8.00	16.00	60.00	275.00
1856*	—	1500.00	2150.00	2500.00	3750.00

*Actually a pattern coin, minted before the law authorizing the issue was enacted.

Indian Head Cent   Minted 1859-1909

	AG	G	GRADES F	XF	MS60
Common Type	.25	.65	1.25	7.50	35.00
Better dates include:					
			Copper-Nickel Variety		
1859	2.00	4.00	10.00	65.00	300.00
1860	2.00	4.00	8.00	25.00	175.00
1861	4.00	8.00	18.00	40.00	250.00
1862	1.50	3.00	5.00	20.00	125.00
1863	1.50	3.00	5.00	20.00	125.00
1864	3.50	7.50	15.00	30.00	200.00
			Bronze Variety		
1864	1.50	3.25	9.00	30.00	90.00
1864*	—	27.50	60.00	150.00	350.00

*The designer's (Longacre) initial appears on the Indian's headdress ribbon.

1865	1.50	3.00	8.00	25.00	75.00
1866	10.00	22.00	35.00	82.00	200.00
1867	10.00	22.00	35.00	80.00	200.00
1868	10.00	22.00	35.00	80.00	200.00
1869	16.00	32.00	68.00	150.00	375.00

1870	12.50	25.00	50.00	100.00	250.00
1871	17.50	35.00	75.00	150.00	300.00
1872	20.00	45.00	80.00	175.00	350.00
1873	5.00	10.00	18.00	50.00	135.00
1874	5.00	10.00	18.00	50.00	100.00
1875	5.00	10.00	18.00	50.00	100.00
1876	5.00	10.00	30.00	75.00	150.00
1877	100.00	200.00	350.00	750.00	1700.00
1878	7.00	15.00	30.00	70.00	150.00
1879	1.50	3.00	8.00	20.00	50.00
1880-1884	.50@	1.50@	4.00@	15.00@	50.00@
1885	1.50	4.00	10.00	30.00	70.00
1886	1.00	2.00	5.00	20.00	65.00
1887-1893	.50@	1.00@	2.25@	9.00@	40.00@
1894	.50	1.25	4.00	9.00	40.00
1895-1909	.25@	.65@	1.25@	7.50@	35.00@
1908S	12.00	20.00	30.00	50.00	150.00
1909S	50.00	100.00	150.00	250.00	425.00

Lincoln Cent   Minted 1909-Date

Lincoln Cent Type
(Wheat Reverse)

Lincoln Cent Type
(Memorial Reverse)

	AG	G	GRADES F	XF	MS60
Common Type	.01	.01	.01	.01	.01

Most all dates and conditions prior to 1959 are worth saving. Commonly called "wheat pennies" because of the wheat ears on the reverse, these cents sell for from $1 to $2 per roll in good or better condition.

In addition, many dates and mint marks bring prices up to $1 or so each. Better coins costing over $1 each in good condition are listed below. Even relatively common dates in high grades command considerable prices.

| | GRADES | | | | |
	AG	G	F	XF	MS60
1909 V.D.B.*	—	2.00	3.00	4.25	12.50
1909S V.D.B.*	—	200.00	250.00	350.00	450.00

*The designer's initials (Victor D. Brenner) are found on the bottom inside rim on the reverse in 1909. They were discontinued from 1909-1917 and replaced below Lincoln's shoulder from 1918 to date.

1909S	15.00	35.00	50.00	80.00	180.00
1910S	2.50	6.50	8.00	15.00	90.00
1911D	1.00	3.00	5.00	22.00	90.00
1911S	4.00	10.00	15.00	25.00	100.00
1912D	1.50	4.00	7.00	30.00	100.00
1912S	4.00	9.00	15.00	30.00	100.00
1913D	.75	2.00	4.00	15.00	67.50
1913S	3.00	7.50	10.00	20.00	100.00
1914D	25.00	60.00	90.00	300.00	900.00
1914S	3.00	8.00	11.00	30.00	150.00
1915S	3.00	7.50	10.00	20.00	100.00
1922**	50.00	125.00	250.00	600.00	2500.00

**No cents minted in Philadelphia. This coin is easily altered. A die for the 1922D cent was faulty.

1922D	1.50	4.00	6.00	16.00	75.00
1923S	.50	1.00	2.50	10.00	150.00
1924D	3.00	8.00	13.00	35.00	200.00
1926S	1.00	2.50	4.00	10.00	100.00
1931D	—	2.00	3.00	7.00	50.00
1931S	—	30.00	33.00	40.00	60.00
1933D	—	1.50	2.00	3.00	20.00

In 1943 the alloy of the Lincoln cent was changed to zinc-coated steel. These coins are easily recognized by their color, ranging from a bright steel to dark steel gray. In 1959 the Lincoln Memorial was placed on the reverse side of the cent to commemorate the 150th anniversary of Lincoln's birth. The coin has undergone further minor modifications since that time. Many other varieties exist due to differing mint mark sizes and metal alloys used. Since 1975, cents minted at San Francisco were produced for proof sets only.

Two-Cent Coins   Minted 1864-1873

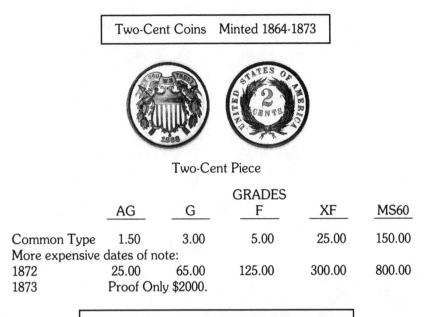

Two-Cent Piece

			GRADES		
	AG	G	F	XF	MS60
Common Type	1.50	3.00	5.00	25.00	150.00
More expensive dates of note:					
1872	25.00	65.00	125.00	300.00	800.00
1873	Proof Only $2000.				

Nickel Three-Cent Coins   Minted 1865-1889

Nickel Three-Cent Piece

			GRADES		
	AG	G	F	XF	MS60
Common Type	1.50	3.50	5.00	13.00	135.00
More expensive dates include:					
1879	15.00	35.00	50.00	75.00	250.00
1880	20.00	50.00	65.00	100.00	300.00
1882	20.00	50.00	65.00	100.00	300.00
1883	35.00	100.00	150.00	250.00	400.00
1884	65.00	200.00	300.00	450.00	600.00
1885	100.00	300.00	400.00	600.00	800.00
1887	65.00	200.00	300.00	450.00	600.00
1888	17.00	40.00	50.00	70.00	300.00
1889	20.00	50.00	65.00	100.00	300.00

1887, 1878 and 1886 exist in proof only and sell in excess of $1,000 each, unless impaired.

Nickel Five-Cent Coins   Minted 1866-Date

Shield Type   Minted 1866-1883

Shield Five-Cent Piece

		GRADES		
	AG	G	F	XF	MS60
Common Type	2.50	6.00	10.00	25.00	125.00
Better dates include:					
1866*	4.00	10.00	18.00	65.00	300.00
1867*	4.00	12.00	25.00	75.00	400.00
*Variety with rays between stars on reverse.					
1871	10.00	25.00	40.00	80.00	270.00
1874	3.00	8.00	12.50	35.00	175.00
1875	3.00	8.00	15.00	40.00	230.00
1876	3.00	8.00	15.00	40.00	200.00
1879	60.00	190.00	300.00	450.00	600.00
1880	70.00	200.00	320.00	450.00	600.00
1881	50.00	160.00	250.00	350.00	500.00

1877 and 1878 were minted in proof only and retail for $1,500-$2,000 each.

Liberty Type   Minted 1883-1913

Liberty Five-Cent Piece

| | | GRADES | | |
	AG	G	F	XF	MS60
Common Type	.25	.50	2.50	7.00	40.00
Better dates include:					
1883 *w/o Cents	1.00	2.00	3.00	7.00	40.00
1883 *w/Cents	2.00	5.00	10.00	25.00	150.00

*Subsequent to the initial strikes the word "cents" was added to the reverse to discourage the passing of gold-plated versions which were more or less easily mistaken for $5 gold pieces.

1885	100.00	210.00	360.00	600.00	1150.00
1886	20.00	40.00	85.00	200.00	450.00
1887-1896	1.00@	3.00@	12.50@	25.00@	130.00@
1897-1899	.30@	.75@	4.00@	15.00@	110.00@
1900-1912	.25@	.70@	2.00@	15.00@	100.00@
1912D	.30	.75	3.00	35.00	265.00
1912S	15.00	35.00	65.00	300.00	600.00
1913	(5 minted. None placed in circulation.) $300,000++				

Buffalo Type   Minted 1913-1938

Buffalo Five-Cent Piece

| | | GRADES | | |
	AG	G	F	XF	MS60
Common Type	.10	.25	.35	2.00	12.00
Better dates (retailing over $1.00 in good condition) include:					
1913*	1.00	2.50	3.00	10.00	25.00
*w/raised ground					
1913D*	2.00	5.00	7.50	20.00	50.00
*w/raised ground					
1913S*	2.50	7.50	15.00	35.00	75.00
*w/raised ground					
1913*	1.00	2.50	3.00	10.00	25.00
*w/o raised ground					
1913D*	10.00	32.00	50.00	88.00	140.00
*w/o raised ground					
1913S*	20.00	60.00	110.00	175.00	300.00
*w/o raised ground					

*Initially the reverse showed the bison on raised ground.

That first year the design was changed removing the ground beneath the bison's feet.

1914	1.00	2.50	4.00	12.00	50.00
1914D	7.00	22.00	40.00	85.00	200.00
1914S	1.50	4.00	7.50	30.00	75.00
1915	.50	1.50	2.50	10.00	35.00
1915D	2.00	5.50	12.50	50.00	115.00
1915S	3.00	9.00	17.50	90.00	150.00
1916D	1.50	4.00	7.50	40.00	110.00
1916S	1.00	2.50	6.00	40.00	110.00
1917D	1.50	4.00	10.00	70.00	175.00
1917S	1.00	3.00	10.00	80.00	175.00
1918D	1.50	4.00	10.00	70.00	250.00
1918S	1.00	3.00	10.00	80.00	200.00
1919D	1.50	4.00	10.00	80.00	300.00
1919S	1.00	3.00	10.00	80.00	300.00
1920D	1.00	3.00	7.50	80.00	300.00
1920S	.75	2.00	6.00	80.00	200.00
1921S	3.00	10.00	33.00	250.00	700.00
1923S	.75	2.00	5.00	50.00	125.00
1924D	.75	2.00	7.50	75.00	200.00
1924S	1.50	4.00	13.00	250.00	750.00
1925D	1.00	3.00	10.00	100.00	250.00
1925S	.75	2.00	5.50	50.00	200.00
1926D	.75	2.00	7.50	100.00	150.00
1926S	1.50	4.00	12.50	250.00	700.00
1927D	.35	1.00	2.50	40.00	80.00
1927S	.35	1.00	2.50	62.50	150.00
1931S	1.00	3.00	5.00	10.00	40.00

Jefferson Type   Minted 1938-Date

Jefferson Five-Cent Piece

	AG	G	GRADES F	XF	MS60
Common Type	.05	.05	.05	.05	.05
Better dates (retailing $1.00 or more in fine condition) include:					
1938D	—	.80	1.00	2.00	4.00
1938S	—	1.25	1.75	3.00	7.00

1939D	—	2.50	3.50	7.50	40.00
1939S	—	.50	1.00	2.00	20.00
1950D	—	—	6.00	7.00	8.00

Set price Circ./Unc./Proof (114 coins): $42.00. Such a reasonable price provides a new collector a good place to begin.

The alloy was changed from 1942-1945 to include 35% silver. Consequently, all "silver nickels" have a value above the common type based on bullion content. (See Chapter 5.) These pieces are distinguishable by color differences (a dirty gray when circulated) and by the placement of a large mint mark at the top reverse position. In MS-60 these coins retail for from $3 to $15 depending on date and mint mark.

From 1971 to date "S" minted coins were produced in proof only. These retail for approximately $1 each.

7
Silver and Clad Coins

In 1966, the United States began minting clad coinage to replace the silver dimes, quarters and half dollars that had circulated for more than 150 years. The effect was immediate, although not noticed by the general public at first. For various reasons many people began looking through their change, taking out the silver coins and putting them away. Some felt that the silver coins would become collectors' items, others feared the end to "hard cash," still others speculated that the rising price of silver would inevitably push up the value of these 90% silver coins. To some extent everybody was right. As silver zoomed to $50/oz. by 1980, tons of coins came out from hiding and headed to the smelter.

Most of the best, however, have been saved for collectors. This chapter offers some assessments of the value of silver coins and the subsequent clad coins that replaced them. Such evaluations are especially tentative given that increases and decreases in the price of silver can affect values so easily. Minimum prices given are predicated on current silver prices—about six times face value. Chapter 5 gives a reasonably complete explanation concerning the refiguring of prices based on changes in the price of silver.

VALUES OF SILVER AND CLAD COINS

Silver Three-Cent Coins   Minted 1851-1873

Silver Three-Cent Piece

	AG	G	GRADES F	XF	MS60
Common Type	3.50	7.50	12.50	45.00	225.00
Better dates include:					
1851O	4.00	10.00	25.00	100.00	400.00
1854	4.00	10.00	25.00	80.00	400.00
1855	6.00	15.00	30.00	125.00	725.00
1856-1858	4.00@	10.00@	16.00@	75.00@	400.00@
1859-1862@	4.00@	10.00@	16.00@	45.00@	250.00@
1863-1872@*	—	—	—	—	600.00@

*Very small quantities minted in these years with few if any reaching circulation. Proofs of these issues retail in the $1,000 range. In 1873 only proofs were minted and currently retail for around $2,000.

The three-cent silver is the smallest U.S. coin minted, very thin, and easily bent. Bent coins command prices considerably less than those listed above.

| Half Dimes   Minted 1794-1873 |

Flowing Hair Type

Draped Bust Type

Draped Bust Type
(Eagle and Shield Reverse)

Capped Bust Type

Liberty Seated Type

		GRADES			
	AG	G	F	XF	MS60
Common Types:					
1794-1795 Flowing Hair	300.00	625.00	1100.00	2600.00	7500.00
1796-1797 Draped Bust	300.00	675.00	1100.00	3000.00	8000.00
1800-1805 Draped Bust					
(Eagle and Shield Reverse)	150.00	525.00	850.00	1250.00	2500.00
1829-1837 Capped Bust	4.00	11.00	22.50	100.00	560.00
1837-1873 Liberty Seated	1.50	4.00	7.50	27.50	250.00

		GRADES		
	AG	G	F	XF	MS60
Better dates include:					
1802	1750.00	3500.00	8000.00	35,000.00	—
1837	8.00	20.00	40.00	175.00	600.00
1838O	25.00	70.00	175.00	700.00	3500.00
1844O	20.00	50.00	125.00	750.00	4000.00
1846	50.00	110.00	225.00	800.00	4000.00
1849O	10.00	25.00	75.00	400.00	2000.00
1853O*	50.00	110.00	225.00	800.00	4000.00

*No arrows at date

> Dimes   Minted 1796-Date

Draped Bust Type

Draped Bust Type
(Eagle and Shield Reverse)

Capped Bust Type

		GRADES		
	AG	G	F	XF	MS60

Common Early Types:

	AG	G	F	XF	MS60
1796-1797 Draped Bust	400.00	800.00	1500.00	3500.00	10,000.00
1798-1807 Draped Bust (Eagle and Shield Reverse)	200.00	500.00	1000.00	1750.00	5000.00
1809-1837 Capped Bust	4.00	10.00	20.00	200.00	900.00

		GRADES		
AG	G	F	XF	MS60

Better date:

	AG	G	F	XF	MS60
1804	400.00	1000.00	2000.00	6000.00	8500.00

Liberty Seated Type   Minted 1837-1891

Liberty Seated Ten-Cent Piece

		GRADES		
AG	G	F	XF	MS60

	AG	G	F	XF	MS60
Common Type	1.00	3.00	7.00	20.00	225.00

Significantly better dates include:

	AG	G	F	XF	MS60
1846	25.00	70.00	115.00	650.00	1200.00
1856S	15.00	40.00	80.00	400.00	1800.00
1858S	15.00	40.00	80.00	400.00	2000.00
1859S	15.00	50.00	110.00	400.00	2000.00
1860O	150.00	300.00	600.00	2000.00	6000.00
1863	20.00	50.00	110.00	250.00	500.00
1864	60.00	150.00	300.00	550.00	1600.00
1865	40.00	100.00	200.00	300.00	600.00
1866	40.00	100.00	200.00	400.00	700.00
1867	50.00	125.00	250.00	550.00	750.00
1868	10.00	25.00	60.00	200.00	500.00
1870S	Only one is known to exist: $150,000 to $200,000.				

Numerous other dates and mint marks retail for prices two to three times the common type prices.

Liberty Head Type   Minted 1892-1916

Liberty Ten-Cent Piece
(Barber)

	AG	G	GRADES F	XF	MS60
Common Type	.60	1.00	2.50	15.00	125.00
Better dates (retailing over $10 in good condition) include:					
1892S	8.00	20.00	30.00	70.00	200.00
1893O	4.00	10.00	20.00	40.00	200.00
1894O	12.00	30.00	60.00	200.00	900.00
1894S	Only 24 known to exist: $50,000.				
1895	20.00	50.00	70.00	150.00	500.00
1895O	50.00	125.00	180.00	375.00	900.00
1895S	5.00	12.50	20.00	50.00	200.00
1896O	15.00	40.00	60.00	125.00	500.00
1896S	10.00	30.00	50.00	110.00	350.00
1897O	10.00	30.00	50.00	150.00	600.00
1901S	10.00	30.00	75.00	175.00	700.00
1903S	8.00	20.00	40.00	110.00	500.00
1904S	6.00	15.00	30.00	110.00	500.00

In lower conditions the issue is sensitive to increases in bullion prices.

Mercury Head Type   Minted 1916-1945

Mercury Ten-Cent Piece

	AG	G	GRADES F	XF	MS60
Common Type	.60	1.00	1.00	2.00	8.00

Significantly higher priced dates include:

	AG	G	F	XF	MS60
1916D	165.00	325.00	700.00	1250.00	2100.00
1921	9.00	18.00	50.00	300.00	700.00
1921D	10.00	25.00	75.00	300.00	700.00
1926S	3.00	7.00	12.50	75.00	400.00
1931D	3.00	7.00	10.00	25.00	75.00

Lower graded coins are bullion sensitive. In higher grades many issues sell in excess of common type prices.

Roosevelt Type   Minted 1946-Date

Roosevelt Ten-Cent Piece

	AG	G	GRADES F	XF	MS60
Common Type*	.50	.60	.60	.80	1.00

  *Silver issues to 1964

Several dates command significantly higher prices in uncirculated grades. These include:

	AG	G	F	XF	MS60
1949	—	—	—	—	9.00
1949S	—	—	—	—	15.00
1950S	—	—	—	—	12.50
1951S	—	—	—	—	8.00

Lower graded coins 1964 and before are bullion sensitive. The non-silver issues (1965-Date) retail for 20 cents each in uncirculated.

From 1968-Date S-mint coins have been minted in proof only. These retail for about $1 each.

Twenty-Cent Coins   Minted 1875-1878

Twenty-Cent Piece

	AG	G	GRADES F	XF	MS60
Common Type	15.00	30.00	55.00	175.00	800.00
Better dates include:					
1875	20.00	50.00	80.00	200.00	1000.00
1875CC	20.00	50.00	80.00	200.00	1000.00
1876	30.00	70.00	125.00	275.00	1100.00

1876CC   About 15 known to exist: $25,000 to $50,000.
1877 and 1878 Exist in proof only and retail for $8,000 to $10,000 each.

Quarter Dollars   Minted 1796-Date

Draped Bust Type

Draped Bust Type
(Eagle and Shield Reverse)

Capped Bust Type

	GRADES				
	AG	G	F	XF	MS60
Common Early Types:					
1796 Draped Bust	1500.00	3100.00	4500.00	12,500.00	23,000.00
1804-1807 Draped Bust (Eagle and Shield Reverse)	100.00	200.00	500.00	1500.00	6000.00
1815-1828 Capped Bust (Motto on Reverse)	20.00	40.00	75.00	500.00	2000.00
1831-1838 Capped Bust (w/o Motto on Reverse)	15.00	30.00	50.00	225.00	1000.00
Better dates include:					
1804	350.00	750.00	2300.00	7500.00	—
1823 and 1837	Very Rare.				

Liberty Seated Type   Minted 1838-1891

Liberty Seated Twenty-Five Cent Piece

	GRADES				
	AG	G	F	XF	MS60
Common Type	3.00	7.50	16.00	50.00	375.00
Significantly better dates include:					
1841	12.00	30.00	110.00	275.00	1000.00
1842	20.00	50.00	125.00	425.00	1500.00
1849O	140.00	325.00	800.00	2500.00	—
1851O	60.00	160.00	425.00	1000.00	2000.00
1852O	80.00	200.00	400.00	1000.00	2000.00
1853*	60.00	160.00	325.00	500.00	2500.00

*Without Arrows

1855O	15.00	40.00	100.00	300.00	1750.00
1855S	15.00	40.00	100.00	300.00	1750.00
1856S	8.00	20.00	40.00	200.00	1000.00
1857S	15.00	40.00	100.00	400.00	1300.00
1858S	10.00	30.00	60.00	350.00	—
1859S	20.00	50.00	125.00	400.00	—
1860S	30.00	75.00	200.00	800.00	1800.00
1861S	8.00	20.00	70.00	275.00	1800.00
1862S	8.00	20.00	70.00	275.00	1800.00
1863	6.00	15.00	25.00	80.00	700.00
1864	8.00	20.00	60.00	160.00	800.00
1864S	35.00	90.00	250.00	900.00	—
1865	12.00	30.00	70.00	210.00	800.00
1865S	12.00	30.00	90.00	300.00	2250.00
1866	One proof known without motto.				
1866*	60.00	150.00	300.00	600.00	1500.00
*With Motto					
1866S	30.00	75.00	180.00	500.00	1700.00
1867	30.00	75.00	180.00	500.00	1100.00
1867S	15.00	40.00	110.00	250.00	1800.00
1868	15.00	40.00	150.00	300.00	800.00
1868S	10.00	25.00	80.00	175.00	1300.00
1869	30.00	75.00	180.00	450.00	1000.00
1869S	10.00	25.00	80.00	180.00	1000.00
1870	8.00	20.00	40.00	125.00	600.00
1870CC	400.00	1050.00	2250.00	4500.00	—
1871CC	160.00	400.00	1000.00	2500.00	—
1871S	40.00	110.00	350.00	800.00	2000.00
1872CC	80.00	200.00	450.00	1500.00	4000.00
1872S	40.00	100.00	300.00	600.00	3000.00
1873CC*	Very Rare: Two are known.				
*Without Arrows					
1873CC*	250.00	500.00	900.00	2250.00	7000.00
*With Arrows					
1875CC	10.00	30.00	100.00	300.00	1500.00
1878S	15.00	40.00	100.00	225.00	1500.00
1879	25.00	60.00	100.00	200.00	550.00
1880	25.00	60.00	100.00	200.00	550.00
1881	25.00	60.00	100.00	200.00	550.00
1882	25.00	60.00	100.00	200.00	500.00
1883	25.00	60.00	100.00	200.00	500.00
1884	30.00	75.00	100.00	200.00	500.00
1885	25.00	60.00	100.00	200.00	500.00
1886	30.00	80.00	110.00	250.00	550.00

1887	25.00	60.00	100.00	200.00	500.00
1888	25.00	60.00	100.00	200.00	500.00
1889	25.00	60.00	100.00	200.00	500.00
1890	15.00	35.00	60.00	120.00	400.00
1891O	40.00	100.00	175.00	500.00	2000.00

Liberty Head Type   Minted 1892-1916

Liberty Twenty-Five Cent Piece
(Barber)

| | GRADES | | | | |
	AG	G	F	XF	MS60
Common Type	1.25	2.25	7.50	40.00	200.00
Significantly better dates (over $10.00 retail in good) include:					
1892S	4.00	12.50	25.00	70.00	350.00
1896S	80.00	200.00	450.00	1200.00	3250.00
1901O	4.00	10.00	25.00	100.00	700.00
1901S	400.00	950.00	1700.00	3300.00	9000.00
1913	4.00	10.00	30.00	300.00	1250.00
1913S	100.00	275.00	500.00	1400.00	3000.00
1914S	4.00	12.50	35.00	200.00	650.00

Lower grade common types are bullion sensitive.

Liberty Standing Type   Minted 1916-1930

Liberty Standing Twenty-Five Cent Piece

	AG	G	GRADES F	XF	MS60
Common Type	1.50	2.00	4.00	21.00	110.00
Significantly better dates include:					
1916	—	900.00	1450.00	1750.00	3000.00
1917*	3.00	8.00	14.00	50.00	165.00
*Bare Breast					
1917D*	4.00	13.00	20.00	100.00	200.00
*Bare Breast					
1917S	4.00	13.00	20.00	100.00	200.00
*Bare Breast					
1917**	3.00	9.00	15.00	35.00	125.00
**Covered Breast					
1917D**	6.00	18.00	40.00	100.00	200.00
**Covered Breast					
1917S**	6.00	18.00	30.00	75.00	175.00
**Covered Breast					
1918	4.00	10.00	20.00	50.00	175.00
1918D	7.00	20.00	40.00	85.00	200.00
1918S	4.00	10.00	20.00	45.00	160.00
1919	10.00	25.00	45.00	70.00	160.00
1919D	15.00	40.00	100.00	225.00	500.00
1919S	15.00	40.00	100.00	225.00	400.00
1920	3.00	9.00	17.50	35.00	160.00
1920D	7.00	22.50	45.00	130.00	200.00
1920S	5.00	13.00	25.00	50.00	160.00
1921	18.00	45.00	110.00	225.00	400.00
1923	3.00	9.00	20.00	40.00	150.00
1923S	40.00	110.00	200.00	350.00	550.00
1924	3.00	9.00	20.00	40.00	150.00
1924D	7.00	22.50	40.00	90.00	150.00
1924S	5.00	14.00	25.00	50.00	160.00
1927S	3.00	10.00	55.00	500.00	1500.00

Lower grade coins are bullion sensitive.

Washington Type   Minted 1932-Date

Washington Twenty-Five Cent Piece   1976 Bicentennial Design

	AG	G	GRADES F	XF	MS60
Common Type (Silver Issues):					
	1.25	1.50	1.50	2.00	2.00
Better dates include:					
1932D	—	30.00	40.00	140.00	400.00
1932S	—	25.00	30.00	45.00	200.00

   In higher grades, most all early coins of the series retail for significantly more than the common type. The non-silver issues (after 1964) have little or no numismatic value. Proofs of S-mint coins (1968-Date) are available for about $1 each. A Bicentennial design is found on the reverse of 1776-1976 dated coins—a Colonial drummer. Uncirculated silver pieces of this date retail for $2; silver proofs for $3.50.

Half Dollars   Minted 1794-Date

Flowing Hair Type

Draped Bust Type
(Eagle and Shield Reverse)

Capped Bust Type

			GRADES		
	AG	G	F	XF	MS60
Common Early Types:					
1794-1795 Flowing Hair	200.00	375.00	675.00	2500.00	—
1796-1797 Draped Bust	6000.00	10,000.00	15,000.00	30,000.00	—
1801-1807 Draped Bust (Eagle and Shield Reverse)	25.00	65.00	150.00	550.00	4200.00
1807-1839 Capped Bust	10.00	20.00	35.00	100.00	800.00
Better Dates:					
1794	500.00	1050.00	2500.00	7000.00	—
1801 & 1802	40.00	125.00	325.00	1300.00	7500.00
1815	300.00	625.00	1000.00	2250.00	6000.00
1836 Reeded Edge	—	300.00	500.00	1600.00	4500.00
1838O			Very Rare.		
1839O	—	125.00	210.00	575.00	4500.00

Liberty Seated Type   Minted 1839-1891

Liberty Seated Fifty-Cent Piece

	AG	G	GRADES F	XF	MS60
Common Type	6.00	14.00	30.00	50.00	400.00

Many dates retail in excess of common date prices. Those selling for over $30.00 in good condition include:

	AG	G	F	XF	MS60
1839	10.00	30.00	70.00	500.00	5000.00
1848	10.00	30.00	55.00	175.00	1000.00
1850	12.50	35.00	100.00	300.00	1250.00
1851	12.50	35.00	100.00	300.00	1250.00
1852	30.00	80.00	225.00	600.00	1750.00
1852O	12.50	35.00	100.00	300.00	1250.00
1853O	Very Rare: Only three known to exist.				
1855S	150.00	300.00	700.00	2700.00	—
1857S	15.00	30.00	75.00	375.00	1500.00
1866*	Only one proof known.				
*Without Motto					
1866S	20.00	40.00	125.00	375.00	5000.00
1870CC	200.00	400.00	1000.00	3300.00	—
1871CC	50.00	100.00	200.00	600.00	3400.00
1872CC	15.00	35.00	100.00	375.00	2000.00
1873CC*	20.00	60.00	175.00	475.00	2550.00
*Without Arrows					
1873CC*	25.00	60.00	175.00	475.00	1850.00
*With Arrows					
1873S*	15.00	35.00	100.00	350.00	1250.00
*With Arrows					
1874CC	50.00	125.00	375.00	1000.00	5000.00
1874S	10.00	30.00	65.00	300.00	1500.00
1878CC	75.00	175.00	400.00	1250.00	2500.00
1878S	1250.00	2500.00	5000.00	8500.00	18,000.00
1879-1890	50.00@	125.00@	200.00@	325.00@	825.00@

Liberty Head Type   Minted 1892-1915

Liberty Fifty-Cent Piece
(Barber)

			GRADES		
	AG	G	F	XF	MS60
Common Type	3.00	5.00	20.00	100.00	450.00
Significantly better dates (over $15.00 in good) include:					
1890O	30.00	90.00	140.00	350.00	800.00
1892S	30.00	90.00	140.00	350.00	800.00
1893S	10.00	35.00	75.00	300.00	800.00
1896S	10.00	35.00	75.00	300.00	1100.00
1897O	10.00	35.00	75.00	525.00	1250.00
1897S	20.00	60.00	125.00	325.00	1250.00
1913	6.00	15.00	30.00	200.00	800.00
1914	6.00	15.00	50.00	250.00	800.00
1915	6.00	15.00	35.00	250.00	800.00

Lower grade coins are bullion sensitive.

Liberty Walking Type   Minted 1916-1947

Liberty Walking Fifty-Cent Piece

		GRADES		
	AG	G	F	XF	MS60

	AG	G	F	XF	MS60
Common Type	3.00	4.00	4.00	8.00	40.00
Significantly better dates (over 10.00 in good) include:					
1916	5.00	15.00	45.00	150.00	400.00
1916D OBV.	5.00	15.00	25.00	125.00	400.00
1916S OBV.	9.00	30.00	95.00	300.00	700.00
1917D OBV.	4.00	12.00	25.00	150.00	400.00
1917S OBV.	5.00	10.00	35.00	300.00	800.00
OBV. = Mint mark on observe					
1919	3.00	10.00	25.00	350.00	1500.00
1919D	3.00	10.00	20.00	350.00	1500.00
1921	20.00	50.00	150.00	1000.00	2000.00
1921D	30.00	75.00	190.00	1000.00	6000.00
1921S	5.00	14.00	35.00	1000.00	6000.00
1938D	10.00	20.00	25.00	85.00	325.00

Lower grades are bullion sensitive. Higher grades of many dates retail in excess of common type prices.

Franklin Type   Minted 1949-1963

Franklin Fifty-Cent Piece

	AG	G	GRADES F	XF	MS60
Common Type	—	3.00	3.00	3.00	6.00

All grades to MS60 are bullion sensitive.

Kennedy Type   Minted 1964-Date

Kennedy Fifty-Cent Piece

1976 Bicentennial Design

		GRADES		
	G	F	XF	MS60
Common Type:				
90% Silver (1964)	—	3.00	3.00	4.00
40% Silver (1965-70)	—	1.50	1.50	2.00
Better dates:				
1970D Issued in mint sets only				20.00

1968S-1969S, Proofs only, $4 each. 1970S Proof $9.00.

Clad S-mint, Proofs only, $1-$5 each.

			GRADES	
		XF	MS60	Proof
1776-1976	Bicentennial Reverse (Independence Hall)			
	Clad	.80	1.00	—
	S-mint Clad	—	—	1.50
	S-mint Silver Clad	—	2.50	4.00

DOLLARS   Minted 1794/1981

Flowing Hair Type

Draped Bust Type

Draped Bust Type
(Eagle and Shield Reverse)

	AG	G	GRADES F	XF	MS60
Common Early Types:					
1794-1795 Flowing Hair	400.00	800.00	1200.00	4000.00	25,000.00
1796-1798 Draped Bust	250.00	600.00	1000.00	3000.00	12,500.00
1798-1803 Draped Bust					
(Eagle and Shield Reverse)	150.00	300.00	500.00	1500.00	9000.00
1836-1839 Gobrecht	Circulated pieces retail for $2500-$5000.				
Better dates include:					
1794	3800.00	6400.00	15,000.00	45,500.00	—
1795 Draped Bust	350.00	700.00	1200.00	3900.00	15,000.00
1798	300.00	850.00	1500.00	5000.00	18,000.00
1804	Very Rare.				

Liberty Seated Type   Minted 1840-1873

Liberty Seated Dollar

	AG	G	GRADES F	XF	MS60
Common Type	25.00	60.00	135.00	300.00	700.00
Better dates include:					
1850	—	225.00	400.00	1000.00	4000.00
1851	—	—	1800.00	4000.00	12,000.00
1852	—	—	—	—	12,000.00
1854	—	350.00	600.00	1500.00	3200.00
1855	—	350.00	600.00	1300.00	3200.00
1861	—	200.00	400.00	800.00	2000.00
1862	—	200.00	350.00	600.00	2000.00
1870CC	—	225.00	400.00	800.00	3250.00
1870S	Very Rare.				
1871CC	—	800.00	2200.00	3500.00	8000.00
1872CC	—	500.00	1000.00	2500.00	5000.00
1873CC	—	1000.00	1500.00	3500.00	15,000.00

Trade Dollar Type   Minted 1873-1885

Trade Dollar

| | | GRADES | | |
	AG	G	F	XF	MS60
Common Type	25.00	50.00	70.00	150.00	500.00
Better date:					
1878S	75.00	150.00	300.00	700.00	4500.00

Proof only issues were minted in Philadelphia from 1878 to 1885. The 1878-1883 issues retail for approximately $3,000. The 1884 and 1885 issues are very rare.

As these dollars circulated in the East they were stamped with Oriental characters called "chop marks." Collectors generally view such pieces as defaced and their value is considerably less than those found above.

Liberty Head Type   Minted 1878/1921

Liberty Head Dollar
(Morgan)

		GRADES		
	AG	G	F	XF	MS60

	AG	G	F	XF	MS60
Common Type	7.00	9.00	10.00	11.00	20.00
Better dates (over $25.00 in good) include:					
1879CC	12.50	25.00	35.00	185.00	1300.00
1880CC	15.00	30.00	43.00	80.00	165.00
1881CC	25.00	55.00	80.00	125.00	250.00
1882CC	12.50	25.00	30.00	50.00	90.00
1883CC	12.50	25.00	30.00	50.00	90.00
1884CC	25.00	55.00	80.00	100.00	125.00
1885CC	75.00	175.00	215.00	230.00	265.00
1889CC	50.00	120.00	160.00	600.00	5500.00
1893	12.50	25.00	40.00	75.00	300.00
1893CC	12.50	30.00	50.00	270.00	700.00
1893O	12.50	25.00	40.00	180.00	1000.00
1893S	250.00	500.00	800.00	3000.00	18,000.00
1894	60.00	150.00	200.00	325.00	1000.00
1895	Very Rare, exists in proof only.				
1895O	15.00	30.00	40.00	170.00	2000.00
1895S	20.00	50.00	70.00	300.00	850.00
1903O	50.00	125.00	160.00	200.00	250.00

Lower grades are bullion sensitive. Higher grades of many dates retail in excess of common type prices.

Peace Type   Minted 1921-1935

Peace Dollar

		GRADES		
	AG	G	F	XF	MS60

	AG	G	F	XF	MS60
Common Type	7.00	9.00	10.00	11.00	20.00
Better dates (over $25.00 in fine) include:					
1921	10.00	20.00	25.00	35.00	200.00
1928	—	65.00	100.00	120.00	200.00

Lower grades are bullion sensitive. Higher grades of many dates retail in excess of common type prices.

Eisenhower Type   Minted 1971/1978

Eisenhower Dollar

1976 Bicentennial Design

Although the coin is rarely seen in circulation, it, nevertheless, carries no premium in those conditions.

Some special mint and proof set issues along with better regular issue dates include:

		GRADES	
		MS60	Proof
1971S	40% Silver	4.00	6.00
1972S	40% Silver	8.00	8.00
1973		4.00	—
1973D		4.00	—
1973S	Clad Proof	—	4.00
1973S	40% Silver	10.00	35.00
1974S	Clad Proof	—	3.00
1974S	40% Silver	9.00	10.00
1976S	Clad Proof	5.00	5.00
1976S	40% Silver	4.00	10.00
1977S	Clad Proof	—	3.00
1978S	Clad Proof	—	3.00

A special Liberty Bell and moon reverse is found on the Bicentennial coins dated 1776-1976.

Anthony Type   Minted 1979-1981

Anthony Dollar

	GRADES			
	F	XF	MS60	Proof
Common Type	1.00	1.00	1.75	7.00

Received very poorly by the public for circulation purposes, quantities of this coin in excess of hundreds of millions remain stored in government vaults.

8
Gold Coins

WHAT ABOUT GOLD COINS?

The U.S. government has minted coins in gold since 1792 (some pattern pieces) when the first authorizing act was passed permitting the mintage of gold coins with the values of $2.50, $5 and $10. Until 1933, when gold coins were discontinued, over four and one-half billion dollars' worth of gold coins had been made. Pursuant to the gold law, many of these were melted down and were for a time stored in bars at Fort Knox.

Naturally, people were quick to ask whether they could still collect gold coins and keep those they already owned. The law made provision for keeping coins of recognized value to collectors which involved dates and mint marks, as well as recognized conditions, like those coins of metals other than gold. Many coins of marginal collector value found their way overseas. With the rise in price of the metal and the loosening of restrictions for Americans who wanted to hold gold, many of these coins have, since 1974, found their way back into the United States.

However, no provision was made for the expanded interest in coin collecting that was due to come. The best way to understand the ramifications of the gold act is to read a copy of the law relating to "Hoarding of Gold," which is given below.

Values of the various dates are covered later in this chapter.

The following is a copy of the law relating to gold coins:

Hoarding of Gold

EXECUTIVE ORDER NO. 6260

Section 4, Acquisition of gold coin and gold bullion.

"No person other than a Federal Reserve bank shall after the date of this order acquire in the United States any gold coin, gold bullion, or gold certificates except under license therefore issued pursuant to this Executive Order, provided that member banks of the Federal Reserve System may accept delivery of such coin, bullion, and certificates, for surrender promptly to a Federal Reserve bank and provided further that persons requiring gold for use in industry, profession or art in which they are regularly engaged may replenish their stocks of gold up to an aggregate amount of $100, by acquisitions of gold bullion held under licenses issued under Section 5 (b), without necessity of obtaining a license for such acquisitions; and provided further that collectors of rare and unusual coin may acquire from one another and hold without necessity of obtaining a license therefore gold coin having a recognized special value to collectors of rare and unusual coin may acquire from one another and hold without necessity of obtaining a license thereof gold coin having a recognized special value to collectors of rare and unusual gold (but not including quarter eagles, otherwise known as $2.50 pieces, unless held, together with rare and unusual coin, as part of a collection for historical, scientific or numismatic purposes, containing not more than four quarter eagles of the same date and design and struck by the same mint)."

On December 31, 1974, the gold law was rescinded after being in effect for a full 40 years. Since that period, the price of gold has soared to many times what it was in 1933, reaching a high of $900/ oz. in early 1980. In a sense, this means that all gold coins could be regarded as collector's items, regardless of rarity or condition. Of course, the fluctuations of the gold market figure in such calculations. Gold would have to sell at about $205 an ounce for U.S. coins to be worth ten times their face value. At the time the above law was written, gold had only approached that figure. A week after the law was rescinded, the U.S. Treasury was accepting all bids of $153 to $185 an ounce, which meant specifically that a $5 gold piece would be worth about $37.50 to $44.75; a $10 gold piece from about $75 to $89.50; and a $20 gold piece from $150 to $179. That, however, applied only to the value of the metal; anyone acquiring gold U.S. coins at those prices could sell them at whatever profit the demand by collectors would bring.

Today a $20 gold piece can be purchased for just a nominal amount above its gold content value. Making such pieces a bargain? Also, more recently, the U.S. government has decided to get back into the gold coin business. It currently has sold a variety of commemorative and bullion gold pieces.

VALUES OF GOLD COINS

Gold Dollars   Minted 1849-1889

Liberty Head Type   Minted 1849-1854

Liberty Head Gold Dollar

	GRADES		
	F	XF	MS60
Common Type	130.00	200.00	750.00

Virtually all mint-marked issues sell for multiples of two to three times the common type price.

Small Indian Head Type   Minted 1854-1856

Indian Head (Small) Gold Dollar

	F	GRADES XF	MS60
Common Type	200.00	500.00	5000.00
Better dates include:			
1855C	650.00	2000.00	7000.00
1855D	1500.00	5500.00	18,000.00

Large Indian Head Type   Minted 1856-1889

Indian Head (Large) Gold Dollar

	F	GRADES XF	MS60
Common Type	135.00	195.00	600.00
Better dates include:			
1856D	2750.00	6000.00	20,000.00
1860D	2000.00	5000.00	17,500.00
1861D	4500.00	7500.00	30,000.00
1875	2000.00	3000.00	8000.00

Many other dates sell for two to three times the common type price.

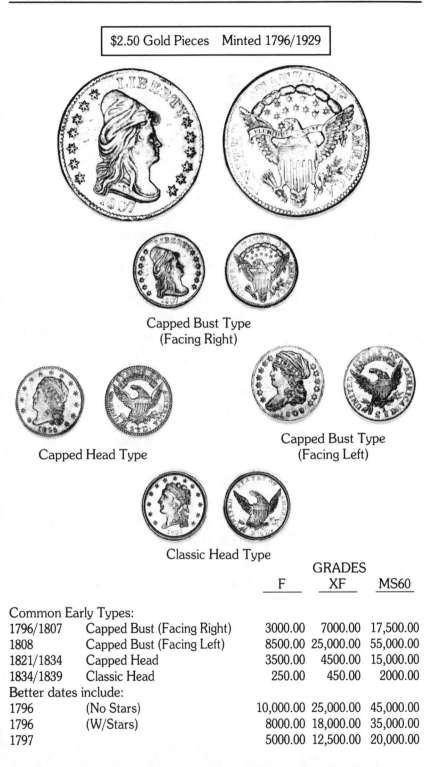

$2.50 Gold Pieces   Minted 1796/1929

Capped Bust Type
(Facing Right)

Capped Head Type

Capped Bust Type
(Facing Left)

Classic Head Type

		GRADES		
		F	XF	MS60
Common Early Types:				
1796/1807	Capped Bust (Facing Right)	3000.00	7000.00	17,500.00
1808	Capped Bust (Facing Left)	8500.00	25,000.00	55,000.00
1821/1834	Capped Head	3500.00	4500.00	15,000.00
1834/1839	Classic Head	250.00	450.00	2000.00
Better dates include:				
1796	(No Stars)	10,000.00	25,000.00	45,000.00
1796	(W/Stars)	8000.00	18,000.00	35,000.00
1797		5000.00	12,500.00	20,000.00

Coronet Type   Minted 1840-1907

Coronet $2.50 Gold Piece

	F	GRADES XF	MS60
Common Type	150.00	225.00	750.00
Better dates include:			
1840D	450.00	3000.00	8000.00
1841	Very Rare.		
1841D	500.00	2750.00	6000.00
1842D	400.00	1500.00	5000.00
1845O	600.00	1750.00	10,000.00
1846C	500.00	1100.00	4000.00
1848 "Cal." on reverse	Very Rare.		
1852D	400.00	1100.00	4000.00
1853D	400.00	1100.00	4000.00
1854D	1200.00	4500.00	10,000.00
1854S	Very Rare.		
1855C	600.00	1800.00	5000.00
1855D	2000.00	4500.00	15,000.00
1856D	3000.00	9000.00	30,000.00
1857D	400.00	1200.00	4500.00
1859D	450.00	1500.00	5000.00
1864	700.00	2500.00	6500.00
1865	700.00	2300.00	6500.00
1875	2000.00	5000.00	12,000.00
1881	600.00	2000.00	5000.00
1885	450.00	1200.00	3000.00

A number of other dates sell for somewhat more than the common type.

Indian Head Type   Minted 1908/1929

Indian Head $2.50 Gold Piece

	F	GRADES XF	MS60
Common Type	175.00	200.00	400.00
Better dates include:			
1911D	500.00	950.00	3000.00

$3.00 Gold Pieces   Minted 1854-1889

Indian Head $3.00 Gold Piece

	F	GRADES XF	MS60
Common Type	400.00	625.00	3000.00
Better dates include:			
1854D	5000.00	12,500.00	40,000.00
1865	700.00	1150.00	6600.00
1870S		One Known.	
1875-1876		Proofs Only—Very Rare.	
1877	750.00	1800.00	6500.00

$4.00 Gold Pieces   Minted 1879-1880

A pattern coin minted in both a Flowing Hair and Coiled Hair type in both years of issue. All pieces are quite rare.

$5.00 Gold Pieces   Minted 1795/1929

Capped Bust Type   Capped Head Type
(Eagle and Shield Reverse)

Classic Head Type

		F	XF	MS60
			GRADES	
Common Early Types:				
1795-1798	Capped Bust	5000.00	12,000.00	25,000.00
1795/1807	Capped Bust			
(Eagle and Shield Reverse)		1200.00	3000.00	10,000.00
1807-1834	Capped Head (Facing Left)	1000.00	3000.00	10,000.00
1834-1838	Classic Head	250.00	550.00	2250.00
Better dates include:				
1797		7500.00	12,000.00	30,000.00
1798		Very Rare.		
1795	Second Type (Eagle and Shield)	5000.00	15,000.00	35,000.00
1815		Very Rare.		
1819		Very Rare.		
1821		3000.00	10,000.00	25,000.00
1822		Extremely Rare.		
1824		5000.00	20,000.00	35,000.00
1825		3000.00	8000.00	25,000.00
1826		—	10,000.00	30,000.00
1827		—	20,000.00	35,000.00
1828		5000.00	20,000.00	35,000.00
1829		Very Rare.		
1832		5000.00	10,000.00	25,000.00
1838C		800.00	3000.00	8000.00
1838D		800.00	2500.00	8000.00

Coronet Type   Minted 1839-1903

Coronet $5.00 Gold Piece

		GRADES	
	F	XF	MS60
Common Type	145.00	175.00	325.00
Better dates include:			
1854S	Very Rare.		
1861C	750.00	2500.00	9000.00
1861D	3000.00	7250.00	25,000.00
1864S	1000.00	2500.00	7000.00

Most dates of the "no motto" variety (to 1866) sell for multiples of two to three times the common type price.

1870CC	1200.00	4000.00	—
1875	Very Rare.		
1878CC	800.00	2800.00	—
1887	Proofs Only $20,000.00		

Indian Head Type   Minted 1908/1929

Indian Head $5.00 Gold Piece

		GRADES	
	F	XF	MS60
Common Type	200.00	235.00	650.00
Better dates include:			
1909O	300.00	850.00	6000.00
1911D	300.00	500.00	4250.00
1929	—	3300.00	6600.00

$10.00 Gold Pieces   Minted 1795/1933

Capped Bust Type
(Eagle and Shield Reverse)

| | | GRADES | |
	F	XF	MS60
Common Early Types:			
1795-1797 Capped Bust	5500.00	12,500.00	33,000.00
1797/1804 Capped Bust			
(Eagle and Shield Reverse)	2000.00	5000.00	16,000.00

Coronet Type   Minted 1838-1907

Coronet $10.00 Gold Piece

| | | GRADES | |
	F	XF	MS60
Common Type (W/Motto on reverse)	200.00	400.00	2500.00
Common Type (No Motto on reverse)	200.00	300.00	500.00
Better dates include:			
1838	550.00	1700.00	10,000.00
1839	400.00	1000.00	6000.00
1840	650.00	1500.00	7500.00
1844	450.00	1100.00	5000.00
1855S	500.00	1250.00	5000.00

1857O	500.00	1000.00	5000.00
1858	—	4500.00	20,000.00
1859O	800.00	3000.00	6000.00
1859S	700.00	1500.00	3700.00
1860S	700.00	1600.00	5500.00
1863	2000.00	3300.00	9500.00
1864	625.00	1500.00	4500.00
1864S	1200.00	3600.00	10,000.00
1865	625.00	1500.00	5000.00
1865S	625.00	1500.00	5000.00
1866S W/O Motto	800.00	2000.00	6000.00
1867S	600.00	2000.00	6000.00
1869	650.00	1800.00	3000.00
1870CC	1100.00	4300.00	—
1871	600.00	1600.00	5000.00
1871CC	600.00	1800.00	4000.00
1872	800.00	2500.00	4500.00
1872CC	600.00	1500.00	4000.00
1873	600.00	2000.00	7000.00
1873CC	500.00	1600.00	6500.00
1875	Very Rare.		
1875CC	600.00	1300.00	3000.00
1876	1700.00	3000.00	9000.00
1876CC	650.00	2000.00	4000.00
1877	1500.00	2500.00	10,000.00
1877CC	800.00	1500.00	4000.00
1878CC	800.00	1800.00	4000.00
1879CC	2000.00	4000.00	12,500.00
1879O	1100.00	3000.00	8000.00
1883O	900.00	2750.00	10,000.00

Indian Head Type   Minted 1907/1933

Indian Head $10.00 Gold Piece

	GRADES		
	F	XF	MS60
Common Type	400.00	475.00	750.00
Better dates include:			
1907 (Wire Rim)	Very Rare.		
1907 (Periods before and			
after motto)	Very Rare.		
1920S	—	8000.00	22,000.00
1930S	—	5000.00	15,000.00
1933	Very Rare.		

$20.00 Gold Piece   Minted 1849-1933

Coronet Type   Minted 1849-1907

Coronet $20.00 Gold Piece

	GRADES		
	F	XF	MS60
Common Type	475.00	550.00	650.00
Better dates include:			
1849	One Known.		
1854O	Very Rare.		
1855O	2000.00	5000.00	—
1856O	Very Rare.		
1859O	1750.00	3000.00	10,000.00
1860O	2400.00	5000.00	10,000.00
1861O	800.00	2500.00	8000.00
1870CC	Very Rare.		
1871CC	1100.00	3000.00	10,000.00
1879O	2000.00	4000.00	11,000.00
1881	1750.00	5300.00	12,500.00
1882	—	9800.00	33,000.00
1883-1884	Proofs Only.		

1885	—	8000.00	21,000.00
1885CC	800.00	1500.00	3700.00
1886	—	9800.00	25,000.00
1887	Proofs Only.		
1891	—	3000.00	9000.00
1891CC	1100.00	2400.00	6000.00
1892	—	1500.00	4500.00

Lower grade coins are bullion sensitive.

Saint-Gaudens Type   Minted 1907-1933

Saint-Gaudens $20.00 Gold Piece

		GRADES	
	F	XF	MS60
Common Type	475.00	550.00	650.00
Better dates include:			
1907 Extremely High Relief Plain Edge		One Known.	
1907 Extremely High Relief Lettered Edge	Extremely Rare.		
1907 High Relief	—	4500.00	8000.00
1920S	—	8000.00	14,000.00
1921	—	9000.00	20,000.00
1927D	Extremely Rare.		
1927S	—	4000.00	8000.00
1929	—	5000.00	10,000.00
1930S	—	9000.00	18,000.00
1931	—	9000.00	15,000.00
1931D	—	9000.00	17,500.00
1932	—	9000.00	18,000.00

Lower grade coins are bullion sensitive.

9
Commemorative Coins

By Act of Congress, the mint over the years has been authorized to issue commemorative coins, each celebrating a current or historic event or honoring an outstanding citizen. Such coins show a great variety of design and inscription. Most would not be recognizable to the general public as legal tender, although some issues were placed in general circulation.

Usually, these coins are offered to the public at a premium over their face value. For example, the Colombian Exposition half dollar was sold for $1 at the World's Columbian Exposition in Chicago during 1893. The fact that the mintage of commemorative coins is usually quite small also is a factor that puts them at a premium with collectors.

Since commemorative coins were generally not issued to circulate, most pieces are well preserved and grade toward the high end of the scale that we have used for previous coins. Consequently, in what follows, pricing for two grades has been used, XF-AU which can even apply to an uncirculated coin that has been knocking around in a desk drawer for a few decades, and MS60, the lowest of the uncirculated grades. As with other coins, high-end uncirculated specimens can easily command prices in excess of 5 to 10 times that of MS60.

For the reader's convenience, all commemorative coins are listed by denomination and date with the exception of recent sets. These are found, unseparated by denomination, at the end of this chapter.

QUARTER DOLLAR

<u>Isabella Quarter</u>

Minted in 1893, this was the first U.S. coin portraying a foreign monarch. The obverse shows Queen Isabella of Spain who helped Columbus finance his voyage of discovery. The reverse displays a kneeling female who represents women's industry.

<u>XF-AU</u>   <u>MS60</u>
$200.00 $500.00

HALF DOLLARS

<u>Columbian Exposition</u>

Issued in 1892 and 1893 in celebration of the 400th anniversary of the discovery of America by Columbus, and the Chicago World's Fair of 1893. The obverse shows a portrait of Columbus; the reverse the ship, *Santa Maria,* spanning the two hemispheres.

	<u>XF-AU</u>	<u>MS60</u>
1892	$20.00	$70.00
1893	$10.00	$65.00

Panama-Pacific

Issued by the Panama-Pacific International Exposition in 1915 to commemorate the completion of the Panama Canal. The obverse shows Columbia. The reverse displays the eagle and shield.

XF-AU   MS60
$225.00 $500.00

Illinois Centennial

Issued in 1918 to commemorate the 100th anniversary of the admission of Illinois into the Union. The obverse shows a bust of Lincoln. The reverse depicts portions of the Illinois state seal.

XF-AU   MS60
$65.00 $125.00

Maine Centennial

Issued in 1920 to commemorate the 100th anniversary of the admission of Maine into the Union. The obverse reproduces the Great Seal of the state. The reverse places the inscription "Maine Centennial, 1820-1920" within a wreath.

XF-AU	MS60
$65.00	$135.00

Pilgrim Tercentenary

Issued in 1920 and 1921 to commemorate the 300th anniversary of the landing of the Pilgrims. The obverse is a portrait of Governor Bradford. The reverse shows the Mayflower.

	XF-AU	MS60
1920 (No Date on Obverse)	$36.00	$55.00
1921 (Date on Obverse)	$80.00	$135.00

Alabama

Issued in 1921 two years late for the 100th anniversary of the admission of Alabama into the Union. The obverse shows the busts of the first (W.W. Bibb) and the then current (T.E. Kilby) governors of the State. Two varieties of the coin exist. The first has the St. Andrews cross between the numbers in "22" (Alabama was the 22nd state) in the field of the obverse behind the governors' heads. The reverse shows an eagle.

	XF-AU	MS60
1921 w/22	$140.00	$350.00
1921 w/o 22	$80.00	$135.00

Missouri Centennial

Issued in 1921 to commemorate the 100th anniversary of Missouri's admission into the Union. The obverse displays the bust of a frontiersman. The reverse shows a standing frontiersman and an Indian.

One variety has a small "2 x 4" on the obverse below the chin of the frontiersman, as Missouri was the 24th state.

	XF-AU	MS60
1921 w/24	$250.00	$500.00
1921 w/o 24	$200.00	$500.00

Grant Memorial

Issued in 1922 to commemorate the 100th anniversary of Grant's birth, the obverse is a bust of Grant. The reverse is a portrait of Grant's log cabin boyhood home.

One variety has a star on the obverse above Grant's last name.

	XF/AU	MS60
1922 w/star	$325.00	$800.00
1922 w/o star	$60.00	$125.00

Monroe Doctrine Centennial

Issued in 1923 to mark the 100th anniversary of the proclamation of the Monroe Doctrine. The obverse shows the busts of Monroe and John Quincy Adams. The reverse shows the Western Hemisphere, the portion of the world the European powers were warned against interfering in.

XF-AU	MS60
$22.00	$60.00

Huguenot-Walloon Tercentenary

Issued in 1924 to commemorate the 300th anniversary of the arrival of the Huguenots and Walloons, Protestant refugees from Belgium. The obverse shows the busts of Admiral Coligny and William the Silent. The reverse depicts the ship, "New Netherland."

XF-AU   MS60
$50.00 $125.00

California Jubilee

Issued in 1925 to commemorate the 75th anniversary of the admission of California into the Union. The obverse shows a kneeling gold miner. The reverse displays the emblem of the state, a California grizzly bear.

XF-AU   MS60
$75.00 $150.00

Lexington-Concord Sesquicentennial

Issued in 1925 to mark the 150th anniversary of these two famous Revolutionary War battles. The obverse bears a portrait of a standing Minute Man. The reverse depicts the Old Belfry in Lexington.

<u>XF-AU</u>	<u>MS60</u>
$30.00	$50.00

Stone Mountain Memorial

Issued in 1925 to raise funds for sculpturing figures of Confederate heroes on Stone Mountain in Georgia. The obverse shows Lee and Jackson on horseback. The reverse has an eagle perched on the mountain.

<u>XF-AU</u>	<u>MS60</u>
$25.00	$50.00

Vancouver Centennial

Issued in 1925 to mark the 100th anniversary of the building of Fort Vancouver. The obverse shows a bust of the builder, Dr. John McLaughlin. The reverse has a frontiersman standing with a rifle. In the background is the old fort and mountains.

XF-AU   MS60
$250.00 $425.00

Sesquicentennial of American Independence

Issued in 1926 to commemorate the 150th anniversary of the signing of the Declaration of Independence. The obverse has busts of Washington and Coolidge facing right. The reverse shows the Liberty Bell.

XF-AU   MS60
$30.00 $50.00

Oregon Trail Memorial

Issued first in 1926, and subsequently in 1928, 1933, 1934, 1936-1939, to commemorate the memory of the pioneers who died along the Oregon Trail. The obverse depicts a covered wagon moving west. The reverse shows an American Indian superimposed on a map of the U.S.

	XF-AU	MS60
1926	$85.00	$120.00
1926 S	$85.00	$120.00
1928	$100.00	$250.00
1933 D	$125.00	$300.00
1934 D	$100.00	$225.00
1936	$90.00	$180.00
1936 S	$125.00	$275.00
1937 D	$100.00	$150.00
1938 P,D,S (Set)	—	$600.00
1939 P,D,S (Set)	—	$1,200.00

Vermont Sesquicentennial

Issued in 1927 to mark the 150th anniversary of the independence of Vermont. The obverse shows the bust of Ira Allen, founder of Vermont. The reverse captures a stalking mountain lion.

XF-AU	MS60
$150.00	$250.00

Hawaiian Sesquicentennial

Issued in 1928 to mark the 150th anniversary of the landing of Captain Cook in the Hawaiian Islands. The obverse carries a bust of Captain Cook. The reverse displays a full-length statue of a native chief.

XF-AU	MS60
$600.00	$1,000.00

Boone Bicentennial

Issued first in 1934 and subsequently through 1938, these coins mark the 100th anniversary of Daniel Boone's birth. The obverse has Boone facing left. The reverse has standing figures of Boone and Chief Black Fish.

	XF-AU	MS60
1934	$100.00	$125.00
1934 P,D,S (Set)	—	$1,000.00
(Actually issued in 1935 Small "1934" on reverse)		
1935 P,D,S	—	$350.00
1936 P,D,S	—	$350.00
1937 P,D,S	—	$700.00
1938 P,D,S	—	$1,300.00

Maryland Tercentenary

Issued in 1934 to commemorate the 300th anniversary of the granting of the original charter of Maryland to Lord Baltimore. The reverse displays Maryland's coat of arms.

XF-AU	MS60
$100.00	$150.00

Texas Centennial

Issued from 1934 through 1938 to commemorate the revolt of Texas from Mexico in 1836. The obverse has an eagle superimposed on the "Lone Star." The reverse contains small portraits of Sam Houston and Stephen Austin flanking a figure of winged Victory.

	XF-AU	MS60
1934	$100.00	$125.00
1935 P,D,S (Set)	—	$425.00
1936 P,D,S (Set)	—	$425.00
1937 P,D,S (Set)	—	$425.00
1938 P,D,S (Set)	—	$800.00

Arkansas Centennial

First issued in 1935, a year before the actual centennial, and then through 1939, these coins commemorate the 100th anniversary of the admission of Arkansas into the Union. The obverse shows a soaring eagle. The reverse the heads of an Indian chief and a then contemporary American girl.

	XF-AU	MS60
Type coin (any year)	$70.00	$95.00
1935 P,D,S (Set)	—	$275.00
1936 P,D,S (Set)	—	$275.00
1937 P,D,S (Set)	—	$275.00
1938 P,D,S (Set)	—	$500.00
1939 P,D,S (Set)	—	$900.00

Connecticut Tercentenary

Issued in 1935 to commemorate the 300th anniversary of the founding of the colony of Connecticut. The obverse bears a standing eagle reminiscent of the Peace Dollar. The reverse bears a representation of the oak tree in Hartford where, according to tradition, the state's charter was hidden from the British governor in 1687.

XF-AU	MS60
$175.00	$280.00

Hudson Sesquicentennial

Issued in 1935 to mark the 150th anniversary of the founding of Hudson, New York. The obverse shows Henry Hudson's ship, the "Half Moon." The seal of the city of Hudson, depicting a mythical sea scene, is found on the reverse.

XF-AU	MS60
$425.00	$600.00

San Diego Exposition

Issued with the dates 1935 and 1936 for the opening of the exposition, the obverse shows a seated female warrior with a bear in the background. The reverse displays the State of California building at the exposition.

	XF-AU	MS60
1935 S	$75.00	$110.00
1936 D	$75.00	$125.00

Spanish Trail

Issued in 1935 to commemorate the 400th anniversary of the blazing of the "Old Spanish Trail" by de Vaca in 1535. The obverse portrays a longhorn cow from the explorer's name. The reverse maps the trail from Florida to Texas on which is superimposed a yucca tree.

XF-AU   MS60
$500.00 $650.00

Albany Charter

Issued in 1936 to mark the 250th anniversary of the charter of the City of Albany, New York. The obverse depicts a beaver at work. The reverse shows Peter Schuyler and Robert Livingston with Governor Dongan of New York after receiving the city's charter.

XF-AU   MS60
$200.00 $275.00

Bridgeport Centennial

Issued in 1936 to commemorate the 100th anniversary of the incorporation of the city of Bridgeport, Connecticut. The obverse shows the portrait of P.T. Barnum, once mayor and Bridgeport's most famous citizen. The reverse shows an eagle about to soar.

XF-AU	MS60
$125.00	$175.00

Cincinnati Music Center

Issued in 1936 to commemorate the 50th anniversary of Cincinnati as a music center. The obverse carries a portrait of Stephen Foster. The reverse shows an allegorical figure representing music.

	XF-AU	MS60
1936 Type single	$250.00	$300.00
1936 P,D,S (Set)	—	$950.00

Cleveland Exposition

Issued in 1936 to mark the 100th anniversary of the founding of Cleveland as part of the Great Lakes Exposition held in Cleveland during that year. The obverse portrays General Moses Cleaveland (old spelling), and ancestor of President Grover Cleveland. The reverse shows a map of nine large cities on the Great Lakes.

XF-AU	MS60
$70.00	$110.00

Columbia Sesquicentennial

Issued in 1936 on the 150th anniversary of the founding of the city of Columbia, South Carolina. The obverse shows justice with sword and scales. The reverse shows a palmetto tree, emblem of the state of South Carolina.

	XF-AU	MS60
1936 type single	$200.00	$300.00
1936 P,D,S (Set)	—	$925.00

Delaware Tercentenary

Issued in 1936 on the 300th anniversary of the landing of Swedish immigrants in Delaware. The obverse shows the Old Swedes Church in Wilmington. The reverse displays the vessel, "Kalmor Nyckel," used for the journey.

XF-AU   MS60
$175.00 $250.00

Elgin Centennial

Issued in 1936 to mark the 100th anniversary of the founding of Elgin, Illinois. The obverse shows a pioneer's portrait. The reverse depicts a Pioneer Memorial Statue to be fashioned from the monies received by the commemorative coin.

XF-AU   MS60
$175.00 $250.00

Gettysburg

Issued in 1936 to commemorate the Battle of Gettysburg. The obverse shows a Union and Confederate soldier. The reverse displays the shields of the Union and Confederacy.

XF-AU   MS60
$175.00 $250.00

Long Island Tercentenary

Issued in 1936 to commemorate the 300th anniversary of the Dutch Settlement of Jamaica Bay, Long Island, New York. The obverse shows a Dutch settler and a native American. A Dutch sailing vessel is depicted on the reverse.

XF-AU   MS60
$60.00 $85.00

Lynchburg Sesquicentennial

Issued in 1936 to mark the 150th anniversary of the charter for Lynchburg, Virginia. The obverse portrays Carter Glass, long-time U.S. Senator from Virginia and Secretary of the Treasury under Woodrow Wilson. The reverse shows Liberty standing before the city courthouse.

XF-AU   MS60
$175.00 $225.00

Norfolk Bicentennial

Issued in 1936 to commemorate the 200th anniversary of the borough of Norfolk. The obverse is a representation of the city's Great Seal. On the reverse is found the Royal Mace of Norfolk.

XF-AU   MS60
$500.00 $550.00

Rhode Island Tercentenary

Issued in 1936 to commemorate the 300th anniversary of the founding of Providence. The obverse shows the founder, Roger Williams, welcomed by a native American. Rhode Island's state motto, "Hope," and an anchor are found on the reverse.

	XF-AU	MS60
1936 Type single	$80.00	$125.00
1936 P,D,S (Set)	—	$375.00

Robinson-Arkansas Centennial

Issued in 1936 to commemorate the 100th anniversary of Arkansas statehood. (See the previous commemoration.) The obverse again shows a soaring eagle. The reverse (even though it contains a portrait, usually considered the mark of the obverse of a coin) depicts then Senator Joseph T. Robinson.

XF-AU	MS60
$80.00	$125.00

San Francisco Bay Bridge

Issued in 1936 to celebrate the opening of the bridge connecting San Francisco to Oakland. The obverse has a California grizzly bear facing front. The reverse shows the bridge—then the world's largest.

XF-AU   MS60
$75.00 $160.00

Wisconsin Centennial

Issued in 1936 to commemorate the 100th anniversary of the Wisconsin Territorial government. The obverse has a badger superimposed over the state emblem. The Territorial Seal, depicting the mining industry, is found on the reverse.

XF-AU   MS60
$185.00 $260.00

York County Tercentenary

Issued in 1936 to commemorate the 300th anniversary of the founding of York County, the first county in Maine. The obverse is of the old fort on the Saco River. The reverse depicts the York County Seal.

XF-AU   MS60
$185.00 $260.00

Antietam

Issued in 1937 for the 75th anniversary of the Battle of Antietam. The obverse shows the opposing commanders of the Civil War battle, Lee and McClellan. The reverse shows a critical objective of the battle, the Burnside Bridge.

XF-AU   MS60
$300.00 $450.00

Roanoke Island

Issued in 1937 to mark the 350th anniversary of the attempt to colonize Roanoke Island, North Carolina. The obverse shows Sir Walter Raleigh who was active in the early attempts to colonize Virginia. The reverse commemorates the birth of Virginia Dare, supposedly the first white person born in the American colonies.

XF-AU
$150.00

MS60
$225.00

New Rochelle

Issued in 1938 to mark the 250th anniversary of the founding of New Rochelle, New York. The obverse shows a calf which was to be given away every year as part of the terms of gaining title to the land. The reverse depicts the fleur-de-lys, the national symbol of France, since it was the French Huguenots who purchased the land.

XF-AU
$360.00

MS60
$425.00

Iowa Centennial

Issued in 1946 to commemorate the 100th anniversary of Iowa's entrance into the Union. The obverse shows the first capitol building in Iowa City. The reverse depicts the state seal.

XF-AU	MS60
$75.00	$120.00

Booker T. Washington Memorial

Issued from 1946 to 1951 to further the views and ideals of this great black American educator. The obverse is the bust of Washington. The reverse has at its center the legend, "From Slave Cabin to Hall of Fame."

	XF-AU	MS60
Single Type Coin	$9.00	$12.00
1946 P,D,S (Set)	—	$35.00
1947 P,D,S (Set)	—	$50.00
1948 P,D,S (Set)	—	$110.00
1949 P,D,S (Set)	—	$140.00
1950 P,D,S (Set)	—	$125.00
1951 P,D,S (Set)	—	$90.00

Washington-Carver

Issued from 1951 to 1954 to honor the memories of two distinguished black Americans, Booker T. Washington and George Washington Carver. The obverse shows the busts of the two men. The reverse is a map of the United States.

	XF-AU	MS60
Single Type Coin	$9.00	$12.00
1951 P,D,S (Set)	—	$85.00
1952 P,D,S (Set)	—	$100.00
1953 P,D,S (Set)	—	$125.00
1954 P,D,S (Set)	—	$90.00

George Washington Memorial

Dated 1982 to commemorate the 150th anniversary of the birth of George Washington, the obverse shows Washington in full uniform mounted on a horse, while the reverse depicts his home at Mt. Vernon, Virginia.

	MS60	Proof
1982 D	$10.00	—
1982 S	—	$10.00

SILVER DOLLAR COMMEMORATIVE

<u>Lafayette Dollar</u>

Issued in 1900 in memory of Lafayette's contributions to the United States during the revolution. The obverse has Washington's profile superimposed over Lafayette's. The reverse is a reproduction of a monument in Paris showing LaFayette astride his horse.

<u>XF-AU</u>
$275.00

<u>MS60</u>
$900.00

EARLY COMMEMORATIVE GOLD COINS

<u>Louisiana Purchase Centennial</u>

Dated 1903 and issued for the Louisiana Purchase Exposition held in St. Louis in 1904. Two obverses exist: One with the bust of Jefferson, the other with that of McKinley. The reverse is the same on both, showing the denomination and dates.

	XF-AU	MS60
$1.00 Gold Both varieties	$350.00	$650.00

Lewis & Clark Centennial

Issued in 1904 and 1905 to mark the 100th anniversary of the exploration by these two famous men. Their portraits appear on the obverse and reverse.

	XF-AU	MS60
$1.00 Gold 1904	$450.00	$1,100.00
$1.00 Gold 1905	$450.00	$1,100.00

Panama-Pacific Exposition

$1.00 Gold $2.50 Gold

$50.00 Gold
(Round)

$50.00 Gold
(Octagonal)

Issued in three denominations to commemorate the opening of the Panama Canal in 1915. The obverse of the $1 coin shows the bust of a canal laborer. The reverse has two dolphins surrounding the denomination. The obverse of the $2.50 coin shows Columbia astride a hippocampus. On the reverse is an eagle facing left.

The $50 coin was issued in both a round and octagonal variety. The obverse of both shows a bust of Minerva. The reverse displays an owl.

	XF-AU	MS60
$1.00 Gold 1915 S	$300.00	$750.00
$2.50 Gold 1915 S	$800.00	$1,750.00
$50.00 Gold 1915 S (Round)	$20,000.00	$30,000.00
$50.00 Gold 1915 S (Octagonal)	$16,000.00	$25,000.00

McKinley Memorial

Dated 1916 and 1917, issued to mark the death of President McKinley and to raise funds for a memorial building at his birthplace, the obverse is a bust of the slain president. The reverse is a replica of the structure to be built in his honor.

	XF-AU	MS60
$1.00 Gold 1916	$325.00	$775.00
$1.00 Gold 1917	$325.00	$775.00

Grant Memorial

Issued in 1922 to commemorate the 100th anniversary of Grant's birth. The obverse and reverse designs are the same as the half dollar. (See the section earlier in this chapter.)

	XF-AU	MS60
$1.00 Gold 1922 w/star	$850.00	$1,200.00
$1.00 Gold 1922 w/o star	$850.00	$1.200.00

Sesquicentennial of American Independence.

Issued in 1926 to commemorate the 150th anniversary of the signing of the Declaration of Independence. The obverse has Liberty holding a scroll of the Declaration of Independence. The reverse shows Independence Hall.

	XF-AU	MS60
$2.50 Gold 1926	$275.00	$575.00

RECENT COMMEMORATIVE SETS

<u>Los Angeles Olympic Commemoratives</u>

1984 PDS $10.00 Gold Olympic Coins

Issued to commemorate the 23rd Olympiad.

	MS60	Proof
1983 P Silver Dollar (Discus Thrower/Eagle)	$25.00	—
1983 D Silver Dollar (Discus Thrower/Eagle)	$50.00	—
1983 S Silver Dollar (Discus Thrower/Eagle)	$40.00	$30.00
1984 P Silver Dollar (Coliseum/Eagle)	$30.00	—
1984 D Silver Dollar (Coliseum/Eagle)	$120.00	—
1984 S Silver Dollar (Coliseum/Eagle)	$75.00	$30.00
1984 P $10.00 Gold (Runners/Eagle)	—	$575.00
1984 S $10.00 Gold (Runners/Eagle)	—	$305.00
1984 D $10.00 Gold (Runners/Eagle)	—	$395.00
1984 W $10.00 Gold (Runners/Eagle)	$275.00	$250.00

Statue of Liberty Commemoratives

1986 Dollar, Half Dollar and $5.00 Statue of Liberty Coins

Issued in 1986 on the 100th anniversary of the giving of the statue by France to the United States.

The half dollar is clad with the obverse showing the statue welcoming a boatload of immigrants. The reverse shows an immigrant family on Ellis Island facing New York City.

The dollar is stuck in .900 fine silver and shows the statue on the obverse. The reverse displays Liberty's torch.

The gold $5 coin has Liberty's face on the obverse. The reverse shows a landing eagle.

	MS60	Proof
1986 D Clad Half	$7.00	—
1986 S Clad Half	—	$9.00
1986 P Silver Dollar	$27.00	—
1986 S Silver Dollar	—	$29.00
1986 W $5.00 Gold	$340.00	$225.00

Constitutional Commemoratives

Issued in 1987 to commemorate the 200th anniversary of the signing of the Constitution. The obverse of the $1 coin features the inscription, "We the People," superimposed on a sheaf of parchment and a quill pen. The reverse shows a cross-section of Americans from the past and present representing our country's political heritage.

The obverse of the $5 gold coin shows an American eagle holding a quill pen. The reverse also displays the pen with a "We the People" inscription.

	MS60	Proof
1987 P Silver Dollar	$23.00	—
1987 S Silver Dollar	—	$27.00
1987 W $5.00 Gold	$145.00	$155.00

It is worth noting that in the case of the $5 gold coin, the prices above are considerably below the original issue prices.

1988 Olympic Commemoratives

Two U. S. coins are currently being minted to commemorate the 1988 Olympics in Seoul, North Korea. The silver $1 coin depicts the passing of the Olympic flame to the Statue of Liberty torch. The reverse shows the Olympic rings. The obverse of the $5 gold coin portrays the Greek goddess of victory and the reverse displays the five Olympic rings above the Olympic flame.

Below are the mint-issue prices for these coins.

	MS60	Proof
1988 Silver Dollar	$27.00	$29.00
1988 $5.00 Gold	$225.00	$235.00

10
Other Special Issues

PROOF COINS AND SETS

Throughout the history of U.S. coinage, the mint has seen fit to issue, for a variety of special purposes, coins that exhibit the highest achievement of the minting process. Until 1936 these "proof" coins, as they were called, were issued sporadically, and usually for the purposes of souvenir presentations and the like. Since 1936, proof sets have been made available for the general public with the exceptions of the years 1943-1949 and 1965-1967. Until 1964 these sets were issued by the Philadelphia mint. Since 1968 they bear the San Francisco mint mark. These recent sets have generally contained only regular issue coins. Special "prestige" sets in 1983, 1984, 1986 and 1987 have included appropriate commemorative coins.

Proof coins are stuck under a process whereby a great deal of care is taken so that each coin is sharply struck with virtually no imperfections or flaws. Each planchet is struck and restruck by highly polished dies so as to guarantee a sharp impression. Proof coins, unless mishandled, often evidence a mirror-like field with frosty surfaces. However, as is the case with regularly issued coins, differences in condition can be found depending on die wear, care in packaging, etc.

Prices for early proof coins are considerable, most often in excess of even the highest uncirculated grades. The sets issued since 1936 undergo periodic large price fluctuations. Currently, they are priced as follows: (Sets since 1955 are usually traded in their original packaging.)

Year	Price	Year	Price
1936	5000.00	1970S	18.00
1937	3500.00	1971S	5.00
1938	1500.00	1972S	5.00
1939	1500.00	1973S	7.00
1940	1200.00	1974S	7.00
1941	1100.00	1975S	15.00
1942	1100.00	1976S 6 pc. set	8.00
1942w/2 5c	1300.00	1976S 3 pc. set	18.00
1950	525.00	1977S	7.00
1951	235.00	1978S	7.00
1952	200.00	1979S	10.00
1953	130.00	1980S	8.00
1954	70.00	1981S	8.00
1955	70.00	982S	6.00
1956	40.00	1983S	12.00
1957	22.00	1983S Prestige	110.00
1958	33.00	1984S	20.00
1959	25.00	1984S Prestige	70.00
1960	22.00	1985S	20.00
1961	19.00	1986S	18.00
1962	19.00	1986S Prestige	55.00
1963	19.00	1987S	13.00
1964	16.00	1987S Prestige	50.00
1968S	6.00	1988S	10.00
1969S	6.00	1988S Prestige	50.00

MINT SETS

Since 1947 official uncirculated sets of coins from each mint have been packaged for sale to collectors. Until 1959 each set contained two examples of each regularly issued coin which were placed in small cardboard holders. This original packaging is important since the "official" mint sets sell for a bit more than privately assembled sets.

Beginning in 1959 uncirculated coin sets come sealed in plastic envelopes and contain only one example of each date and mint mark.

Only in the years 1965 through 1967 has any special care been taken by the mint to insure that better quality coins were used to make up the sets. This was likely done in lieu of proof sets which were not produced in those years.

1947 PDS	700.00	1968 PDS	4.00
1948 PDS	200.00	1969 PDS	4.00
1949 PDS	600.00	1970 PDS	18.00

1951 PDS	300.00	1971 PDS	4.00
1952 PDS	200.00	1972 PDS	4.00
1953 PDS	175.00	1973 PDS	11.00
1954 PDS	140.00	1974 PDS	6.00
1955 PDS	85.00	1975 PD	6.00
1956 PD	75.00	1976 PD	7.00
1957 PD	100.00	1976 3 pc. set	12.00
1958 PD	90.00	1977 PD	8.00
1959 PD	25.00	1978 PD	6.00
1960 PD	20.00	1979 PD	6.00
1961 PD	20.00	1980 PDS	7.00
1962 PD	20.00	1981 PDS	11.00
1963 PD	17.00	1984 PD	6.00
1964 PD	15.00	1985 PD	10.00
1965	5.00	1986 PD	9.00
1966	5.00	1987 PD	8.00
1967	6.00	1988 PD	8.00

Official order forms for the purchase of Uncirculated Mint Sets can be had by writing: Customer Service Center, The United States Mint, 1001 Aerospace Road, Lenham, MD 20706. A customer service number is listed as: (301) 436-7400.

U.S. BULLION COINS

Gold

Since 1986 the United States has minted gold pieces in various denominations called Eagles to compete with similar bullion coins issued by other countries such as South Africa (Krugerrand) and Canada (Maple Leaf).

These pieces have not been minted in order to circulate but rather to provide convenient units of value for the possession of the precious metal. However, the coins are denominated and, presumably, are legal tender.

The obverse of all four denominations is reminiscent of the $20 Saint-Gaudens gold piece issued until 1933. The reverse shows an eagle landing on the nest.

Year	Denomination	Size	MS60	Proof
1986	5.00	1/10 oz.	Spot + 10%	—
1986	10.00	1/4 oz.	Spot + 9%	—
1986	25.00	1/2 oz.	Spot + 8%	—
1986	50.00	1 oz.	Spot + 5%	—
1986W	50.00	1 oz.	—	525.00
1987	5.00	1/10 oz.	Spot + 10%	—
1987	10.00	1/4 oz.	Spot + 9%	—
1987	25.00	1/2 oz.	Spot + 8%	—
1987W	25.00	1/2 oz.	—	325.00
1987	50.00	1 oz.	Spot + 5%	—
1987W	50.00	1 oz.	—	625.00
1988	5.00	1/10 oz.	Spot + 10%	—
1988W	5.00	1/10 oz.	—	75.00
1988	10.00	1/4 oz.	Spot + 9%	—
1988W	10.00	1/4 oz.	—	200.00
1988	25.00	1/2 oz.	Spot + 8%	—
1988W	25.00	1/2 oz.	—	350.00
1988	50.00	1 oz.	Spot + 5%	—
1988W	50.00	1 oz.	—	650.00

Silver

The one-ounce silver bullion coin is denominated "One Dollar." The obverse is a design virtually identical to the Liberty Walking half dollar last issued in 1947. The reverse displays the eagle with shield. Thus the coin is nicknamed the "silver eagle."

Year	Denomination	MS60	Proof
1986	1.00	13.00	—
1986S	1.00	—	30.00
1987	1.00	Spot + 1.50	—
1987S	1.00	—	20.00
1988	1.00	Spot + 1.50	—
1988S	1.00	—	40.00

Bullion coins cannot be ordered directly from the mint. Over 1,000 outlets are listed in a special mint publication entitled, "American Eagle Buyer's Guide." This brochure can be acquired by calling 1-800-USA-GOLD. Also, the order form for U.S. Mint Sets mentioned above has a section for requesting the brochure by mail.

Recent provisions in the federal tax law allow for the inclusion of the American Eagle bullion coins in a qualified Individual Retirement Account. They are the only tangible asset permitted by law in an IRA.

U.S. GOLD BULLION MEDAL/COINS

The original attempt by the U.S. Government to compete for the millions of dollars that were being used to purchase foreign bullion gold coins was to issue the American Arts Gold Medallion.

Complicated ordering procedures, medal-like appearance and the lack of legal tender status doomed the project almost from the start.

The medallions honored various persons from the arts, writers, etc. Issued in one-ounce and half-ounce sizes, the series lasted from 1980-1984.

Year	Size	Obverse Portrait	Mint State
1980	1/2 oz.	Marian Anderson	250.00
1981	1/2 oz.	Willa Cather	250.00
1982	1/2 oz.	Frank Lloyd Wright	275.00
1983	1/2 oz.	Alexander Calder	450.00
1984	1/2 oz.	John Steinbeck	350.00
1980	1 oz.	Grant Wood	500.00
1981	1 oz.	Mark Twain	500.00
1982	1 oz.	Louis Armstrong	500.00
1983	1 oz.	Robert Frost	500.00
1984	1 oz.	Helen Hayes	575.00

The price of medallions are, of course, bullion sensitive.

11
Where To Find Coins

Was it easier to find interesting coins in circulation years ago? I have to think it was. In 1960, when I first began collecting, there was a much wider range of dates on coins in circulation. One could still find an occasional Indian Head cent or other coins dated before 1900. Almost all Lincoln cents could be found with a good deal of patience. Silver dollars from 1878 to 1935 were available at the local bank. No one seemed to want to carry them as they were quite hard on pockets.

When my paper route no longer provided me with enough change to search for that elusive complete set, I can recall riding my bicycle to the neighborhood savings & loan to obtain a bag (or two since it made more sense in terms of balance) of pennies ($50, 100 rolls, 35 lbs.)! I would bring these home to search for the dates I needed. Then, about 100 Lincoln cents dated from 1909-1960 were needed to complete the set.

Every so often a coin with a retail value of several dollars would be found. You can imagine that one such find alone was enough to guarantee another trip to transact a trade for an additional bag!

In one sense, it is amazing how patient my local banks were at the time. For them no profit was derived by catering to my desires. But even more amazed, as I think back, must have been my parents when their son would be found occasionally searching through a bag of fifty-cent pieces. One thousand dollars would have been transported without benefit of an armed guard to the family kitchen table. There is something to be said for having one's entire fortune within one's immediate grasp.

Those days are gone. Virtually every coin I touched then now sells for a premium over face, albeit in most cases a small one.

Are there finds that can be made today from pocket change or an occasional trip to the bank? Probably not. There are reports from lucky collectors who have been fortunate enough to have found a coin or two probably spent by a child from a parent's collection. Then, too, sometimes some silver coins get rolled up and deposited by someone unaware of their value. But I have to think such occurrences are extremely rare these days.

Coins in circulation, however, still provide a place to start. Try this experiment. Save your pocket change for several months. Then take out all the coins you have saved some evening to see what might be there. You can probably find most cents minted for circulation since 1959. You will find an array of Jefferson nickels from the 1950s through the 1980s, dimes and quarters from 1965 to 1989. No halves or dollar coins, although the bank may have a few. No Lincoln wheat pennies (before 1958), and, alas, no silver!

An error coin or two may come your way. A slightly double-struck coin, or one with a minute die crack may pique your interest along the lines of errors, freaks, and other oddities.

But at least you now have some idea of what is available from this source and what is not. That's the bad news. The good news is that many other coins can be obtained for a minimal amount over face. Their cost is so reasonable that it would have hardly made sense to search the coins in circulation for them.

Other more fruitful places to continue your search might be desks or bureau drawers and jewelry boxes. Almost everyone during their lifetime has set aside an interesting coin or two, received as a gift or kept as a little memento of an event now long forgotten. You will do well to ask other family members or friends concerning such small keepsakes. In most cases there will be an emotional attachment to the item, but at least you might persuade the owner to let you find out about the coin. In some cases, since the value will be minimal, the owner may well decide that your new-found appreciation deserves to be encouraged. My father's cousin once gave me two nickel three-cent pieces on the condition that I would never sell them. Their value was quite small. But at the time, the sheer weirdness of such a coin opened up brand new avenues of awareness in my collecting.

Metal detecting is undoubtedly a hobby in its own right. But the obvious connection to coin collecting is evident with that initial find of a coin that is apparently one not currently found in circulation. Hobbyists of this ilk may soon find themselves researching county records that provide clues as to the sites of previous schools, businesses, and industries. The grounds of such places provide the opportunity to unearth coins that may be quite old, lost by playing children or customers and employees in a rush.

These more solitary pursuits, while rewarding, can take you only so far.

I recommend your next source be other collectors. Contact a family member whom you know is a collector or attend the next meeting of your local coin club. Initially, keep your purchases to a minimum. Compare prices. Talk to other collectors. Nothing discourages the desire to collect coins more than overpaying for the first few of them.

At about this time take a subscription to a numismatic paper or magazine. Get an idea of what is available, prices, condition, terms, etc., from the many ads that appear there. Spend your first $50 on books about coins.

Every collector has more duplicates than he or she will ever need. You may begin by buying a few wheat pennies or a circulated silver dollar or two. Your accumulation will grow surprisingly fast. But don't let it run too far ahead of your accumulation of information. Research your purchases. Find out everything you can about the peculiarities of each coin. Learn about where and how and why it was minted. Develop a consciousness with regard to its value.

Other collectors cannot always provide the specific coins that you may wish to acquire. At that time you may wish to enlist the services of a dealer. There are thousands out there to help you. Some are willing to educate you as you make purchases, some are not. And, of course, as is possible in any business dealing, the opportunity to make a really poor purchase is forever lurking out there. In Chapter 13, I shall discuss in more detail suggestions for buying coins. There are some obvious things to do and avoid.

One last source, more for the acquisition of newly minted and specially struck coins, is the U.S. Mint itself.

Over the last several years the Mint has struck coins commemorating the 250th anniversary of Washington's birth (a half dollar in 1982), the 1984 Olympic Games ($1 and $10 gold coin), the 200th anniversary of the Statue of Liberty (a half dollar, $1, and $5 gold coin in 1986), and the 200th anniversary of the Constitution ($1 and $5 gold coin in 1987).

1988 U.S. Olympic coins to commemorate the Summer Games in Korea are currently available (a silver dollar and $5 gold coin).

In addition, each year the Mint issues proof and mint sets along the lines of coins placed in general circulation for that year (some with special mint marks), various dated bullion coins, and even a number of medals (see Chapter 10).

12
Starting a Collection

SOME POPULAR WAYS OF COLLECTING

Many people who refer to themselves as "coin collectors" are really coin accumulators. I suppose this happens to most of us simply because we have no clear plan for the direction we want our collecting to take. We change our mind concerning what interests us. We tend to buy what is available or offered without much thought as to the scope of what we want to achieve.

A collection presumes order and direction toward a certain degree of completeness. Collecting by date and mint mark has traditionally been a way to assemble 19th and 20th century series.

For example, a Jefferson nickel set is composed of 131 pieces dated from 1938 to 1987. The "S" mintmarked coins from 1968 to the present exist only in proof and, therefore, must come from the proof sets of those years. They are not expensive but since they were not struck for circulation, acquiring them demands a purchase.

Throughout the rest of the set, there are just a few key dates. However, no coin retails for more than $7 in circulated condition. The entire set retails for about $42 although such a purchase would short-circuit the pleasure of assembling the set piece by piece. Also lost would be the knowledge acquired as an accidental feature of checking mintages and seeing the variety of conditions and pricing available.

More often today, collectors are more interested in acquiring coins by type, if for no other reason than the high cost of assembling every date and/ or mint mark of some series. Essentially, this means picking a representative coin from each of the various series minted. Some series have fairly substantial design changes within them, so some decisions have to be made concerning how major such a change must be in order for the coin to be considered a different type. Changes in alloy complicate the matter also. The definition of the "type" might have broadened to include such changes.

A complete set of 20th century type coins (excluding gold coins) would make an interesting and fairly challenging "starter" type set. Such a set would include:

$ .01 Indian (dated after 1899)
$ .01 Lincoln (wheat reverse before 1959)
$ .01 Lincoln (zinc-coated steel, 1943)
$ .01 Lincoln (cartridge case alloy, 1944-46)
$ .01 Lincoln (Memorial reverse after 1958)
$ .01 Lincoln (copper-plated zinc, 1982-87)
$ .05 Liberty (dated after 1899)
$ .05 Buffalo (raised ground, 1913)
$ .05 Buffalo (non-raised ground, 1913-1938)
$ .05 Jefferson (copper-nickel alloy)
$ .05 Jefferson (copper-silver alloy, 1942-45)
$ .10 Barber (dated after 1899)
$ .10 Mercury (1916-1945)
$ .10 Roosevelt (90% silver, 1946-1964)
$ .10 Roosevelt (clad 1965-date)
$ .25 Barber (dated after 1899)
$ .25 Standing Liberty (1916-1917)
$ .25 Standing Liberty (redesigned, 1917-1930)
$ .25 Washington (90% silver 1932-1964)
$ .25 Washington (clad 1965-date)
$ .25 Washington (Bicentennial design dated 1776-1976, clad and 40% silver)
$ .50 Barber (dated after 1899)
$ .50 Walking Liberty (1916-1947)
$ .50 Franklin (1948-1963)
$ .50 Kennedy (90% silver, 1964)
$ .50 Kennedy (40% silver, 1965-1970)
$ .50 Kennedy (clad, 1971-date)
$ .50 Kennedy (Bicentennial design dated 1776-1976, clad and 40% silver)
$1.00 Morgan (dated after 1899)
$1.00 Peace (1921-1935)
$1.00 Eisenhower (1971-1978)
$1.00 Eisenhower (1971-1978, 40% silver)
$1.00 Eisenhower (Bicentennial design dated 1776-1976, clad and 40% silver)
$1.00 Anthony (1979-1981)

The alloy differences might well be ignored making for complete sets of considerably fewer coins.

A much more expensive, although not difficult, challenge would involve collecting an example of each *denomination* of coin that has been minted—half cent to $20 gold. (15 coins in all).

BASIC COIN KNOWLEDGE

However, no matter what directions your collecting interests take you, the most important thing you can do is to keep your knowledge of coins apace with the monies spent on the coins themselves. Put together a small library as you go. Essential are the following:

1. A book on grading coins.
2. A comprehensive catalogue.
3. A comprehensive almanac and history of U.S. coinage.
4. A weekly or monthly paper or magazine.
5. A volume on the aesthetic considerations of U.S. coins.
6. A volume on coin investing.

The following is a list of sources that would be suitable for such a beginning library: One item in each category.

1. *Official American Numismatic Association Grading Standards For United States Coins.* Kenneth Bresset and A Kosoff. Western Publishing, Racine, WI. (1987). Price: $7.95
2. *A Guide Book of United States Coins.* R.S. Yeoman. Western Publishing Co., Racine WI. Commonly referred to as the "Redbook," this catalogue has been published every year since 1947. Price: $6.95
3. *Coin World Almanac.* The editors of *Coin World,* Amos Press, Sidney, OH. (Fifth edition, 1987). Price: $14.95
4. *Coin World,* P.O. Box 150, Sidney, OH 45365. (weekly) Price: $26/year.
5. *Numismatic Art In America.* Cornelius Vermeule. Belknap Press of Harvard University Press, Cambridge, MA. (1971).
6. *High Profits From Rare Coin Investment.* Q. David Bowers. Bowers and Merena Galleries Inc., Wolfeboro, NH. (1983). Price: $14.95

A much more extensive list of sources of information will be found in Chapter 16.

COIN SUPPLIES AND ACCESSORIES

The coin board is an ingenious and inexpensive device for helping you bring some order to your ever larger collection. The task of filling the holes is at once finite and seductive. The most basic kind of coin board or folder costs about $1.50. Prices for more elaborate ones, usually purchased for better grade coins, can range up to $10 and even $50 for some of the fancy plastic holders.

Keeping track of duplicates and other coins you want to save can be done in a variety of ways. Small 2″ x 2″ coin envelopes and several styles of transparent holders are available. The most recent of these is called a "vinyl flip," actually two adjoining clear pockets, one for the coin, another for inserting a small sheet for descriptions and pricing information. Retail they cost from $20-$30/1,000. Any of the above can be placed in specially made vinyl sheets or coin boxes.

Plastic tubes can be purchased to hold rolls or part rolls of coins of current denominations. These are priced at $.15 to $.25 each.

A good 10- or 20-power magnifying glass is a must for any sort of precise grading.

13
How To Buy Coins

COIN SHOPS AND COIN SHOWS

A collector's first exposure to someone from whom he will buy coins in any systematic way is likely be his neighborhood coin dealer. Most coin shops these days have diversified into other collectibles including stamps, baseball cards, political buttons, and almost anything else you can think of. Some may even remind you more of precious metal and money exchanges. A few do considerable business in gold and silver jewelry.

With all this in mind, it is no wonder that a first experience with a coin dealer can be somewhat disappointing. If he is busy selling 10-ounce silver bars he may have little patience with a collector who wishes to pursue his stock of late date Lincolns. Don't be discouraged. Visit several shops. You will eventually find a dealer who is interested in bringing you along as a collector and customer.

Plan to educate yourself as you proceed to buy coins in his shop. Ask questions about grading standards. Compare prices.

If a dealer does not have the coin you are looking for in stock, suggest that he attempt to find one for you. Once you are reasonably comfortable with a particular dealer, you might even supply him with a small want list of coins you are very interested in buying. Good etiquette demands that you give such a list to only one dealer at a time, since he will presume that if the coin meets your standards you will very likely purchase it. Obviously, you would not likely intend to purchase the same coin from several dealers.

Dealers are constantly purchasing collections. So there is never a reason to buy a coin that you are not completely satisfied with. Be patient. That next collection may hold exactly the coin you are seeking.

Other collectors will also likely be willing to sell coins to you from time to time. And clearly you should be able to get a somewhat better price from a collector since he does not incur a dealer's usual costs of doing business.

Paying that lesser price, however, is a two-edged sword. Most collectors will be less willing than a dealer to allow you to return purchases. Also, you will not have near the leverage to satisfactorily clear up any dispute that may arise concerning a purchase. The law looks differently at private party transactions. You will do well to make very clear the conditions for the return of any coins sold to you.

Once you become a bonafide member of your local coin club, the club itself will open to you a variety of ways to purchase coins.

Other members can offer you duplicate coins from their particular specialty that even many dealers would have in stock on only a sporadic basis.

Some members will, in fact, be part-time dealers, sometimes called "vest-pocket" dealers. They will have no shop, maybe no business cards or pricelists. Seldom will they have a retail sales license. The commodity they are selling is price. Often coins can be purchased from an entrepreneur of this sort at or near the prevailing dealer "buy prices" (see Chapter 5 for a discussion and explanation of prices).

Making deals in such circles is probably best conducted by an experienced collector. A vest-pocket dealer, given his small markups, is considerably less inclined to spend a great deal of time educating his customer. At the prices he charges he can just as easily sell to a dealer and minimize any problems that arise due to the ignorance of the prospective buyer.

Coin clubs will also sponsor bourses, where several, and sometimes up to hundreds of dealers are invited to set up tables and display their coins for sale.

Regular lists of the dates of these events are published in most coin papers. The benefits to the collector are obvious. Having so many dealers available makes for a much more efficient way to search for coins and coin knowledge.

Your first visit to a large "coin show," as they are sometimes called, will likely be an overwhelming experience. Millions of dollars worth of coins piled in display trays, bags of coins on the floor behind dealer tables, the unusual racket made by a machine counting junk silver, armed guards everywhere are just some of the things you will see and hear. And here you will be looking for a 1950D nickel!

But don't return to your car in embarrassment. There will be someone on the floor to help you. Take your time. Get acquainted with a few dealers from your area. You may want to visit their shops at a later date, since in this environment it may be difficult to ask all the questions you want. Also, these dealers may very well have other things to show you that they did not bring along.

Peruse the tables to get a sense of grading and pricing by the various dealers. You will undoubtedly be startled by huge discrepancies on both counts.

BUYING BY MAIL

For collectors who live in areas where there are no local dealers, and coin shows are quite difficult to attend, buying coins by mail is a relatively painless alternative.

Coin magazines and newspapers are filled with ads for every conceivable coin. Read them carefully and compare. Be aware of the terms. These will include costs for postage and handling, appropriate sales taxes, return privileges, the manner in which payment should be made, etc. Often a toll-free number will be listed for convenience in ordering.

Since there can be a considerable delay between the time an ad is placed and the time it actually appears in print, it usually does not hurt to confirm the prices of coins that may be of interest. This would be especially true of coins whose prices are bullion sensitive.

You may also wish to take notice of the professional organizations to which a dealer belongs. Membership is often prominently displayed in an ad. And such may well provide a safety net for any disputes that may arise concerning transactions.

A significant drawback to buying by mail is having to buy sight unseen. This problem is magnified with an initial purchase since grading standards vary so. Showing a coin around to collector friends for other opinions makes sense. Trial and error adds to the expense of buying. But there is no real substitute for it.

Asking another dealer for an opinion concerning a coin you have bought by mail is somewhat more problematic. I think it puts a dealer on the spot and I do not recommend it for that reason. Any negative remark could be construed as sour grapes, as in, "Why not buy this coin from me?" On the other hand, positive comments could well be interpreted as encouragement to continue dealing with the other firm. What dealer wants to be put in such a dilemma?

Returning coins purchased by mail is not an inexpensive proposition, although the costs would certainly be less than a drive to the local coin shop.

The U.S. Postal Service offers two ways to protect yourself in mailing shipments of value. Postal "insurance" can be purchased in various increments to $500. The top category costs $5 plus postage. Registered mail runs $4.85 plus postage for $500 and shipments of considerable value (up to $25,000) can be fully covered.

It is not quite clear what the difference is between the two services on amounts up to $500 (except the price, of course). I have had no difficulty collecting under either service. My experience has been that less than one in

1000 packages/letters has been lost or damaged. Both services are very reliable.

Returning or sending coins via certified mail makes no sense, although I know it is occasionally done. No insurance claim can be made for such delivery. "Certified" merely means that the delivery will be signed for. If it is damaged or lost, the sender has little or no recourse.

Other carriers, Federal Express, Puralator Courier, etc., will carry numismatic packages, but the insured limits are quite low, ranging from $50 to $500.

U.P.S. will not be liable for shipments of numismatic items (rare coins) or gold and silver bullion. These terms seem to permit the insured shipment of pennies and nickels having no numismatic value. Presumably, one could ship a bag of wheat pennies and recover at least the $50 face value should they be lost.

MAIL BID SALES AND AUCTIONS

Other popular ways to purchase coins include mail bid sales and auctions.

A mail bid sale allows a bidder to make an offer on a coin within the limits of any minimum bid. Some terms permit the seller to refuse all offers if he so chooses. Also, it may well be the case that some or all the lots are the property of the firm holding the sale. In other words, no consignments have been made to the firm by third parties.

Auctions are quite similar to mail bid sales, except that with an auction the presumption is usually that the coin will be sold to the highest bidder over the minimum. And although some lots may be owned by the auction house, most are the property of the parties who have agreed to pay a commission (usually 10%) to have their coins described, catalogued, and sold. The buyer will also have a 10% commission added to the hammer price.

Auctions are typically designed to handle more expensive properties. In fact, major rarities often cannot be purchased in any other way. Terms vary from auction house to auction house. Great care should be exercised in submitting bids. They are binding and mistakes can be quite expensive.

Being present at an auction can be very exciting, especially if one is attempting to acquire a special, long sought after coin. The emotion of little bidding wars can easily catch up the most phlegmatic.

The purchase of common coins is more easily accomplished by a method of outright purchase. However, good bargains can be found at auction and a familiarity with prices realized is valuable information since it represents actual prices for which coins are trading—information to which a collector would normally have little access.

BUYING DIRECTLY FROM THE MINT

The U.S. Government has become the biggest dealer in the country. So, I suppose, no discussion of how and where to buy coins would be complete unless mention was made of this source.

Should you wish to purchase current mint or proof sets, bullion coins, medals, etc., you will find below an address where you can write to obtain the latest information on products available from the mint.

Write:
  U.S. Mint
  Box 8666
  Philadelphia, PA 19101

In some cases a healthy premium over face value makes up the bulk of the price for the Mint's products. Some recent proof sets currently trade for less than the original price from the Mint. (The 1982 set, for instance, had an original issue price of $11. It currently sells for $8 retail.) So going to "the source" is no guarantee of preservation of value or price appreciation.

Banks and other firms have recently become vendors for Mint products. A trip to your local bank may afford you the chance to see what it is that you might like to purchase. Returns to the Mint are not easily made or even possible in some cases.

MASS-MARKETED AND PROMOTED COINS

As a note of caution, any number of firms have mounted campaigns to mass-market certain coins. Ads in popular, large circulation magazines and papers tout coins as sure-fire investments and sometimes attempt to leave the impression that the firm is some type of official issuing agency. The appeal of such ads is undoubtedly directed to the undereducated collector. I know of no serious collector who would even think of purchasing coins from such sources. Overpricing and overgrading seem to be the rule in this arena. I cannot stress too much the need for the exercise of extreme caution here. I have seen instances of common silver dollars being offered for $25 each as "limited issues" when they were available at every coin shop for around $10. And worse, some "coins" offered never even experienced one transaction on a secondary market. They truly became "dead" issues.

All the more reason to join a coin club. Ask other members' opinions regarding such issues. Get a good idea about price *before* you buy that first coin.

14
How To Sell Coins

A DAY IN THE LIFE OF A DEALER

To understand some of the dimensions of selling the coins we may have lovingly amassed over a lifetime, let us sit with a dealer through a typical day. Such knowledge may also have an impact on how we go about assembling our collection from the start.

Unlike you, a dealer need not be in love with the coins he buys. This gives him or her an entirely different attitude in any transaction. When he looks at the "deal," he wants to be virtually assured that a profit can be made. He must "feed" every coin until the day it is sold. Since his living is based on his judgments, he must "live" with his mistakes in a different way than a collector does.

For some dealers this means making the absolutely lowest offer for a collection that he thinks the seller might accept. Ethics aside, this works sometimes and indeed there are at least some positive things that can be said about such a strategy. I am not recommending this approach and I shall say more about it later.

Well what can a collector expect? The person on the other side of the counter has been in the office since 9 a.m. In the next few hours several calls will be received that are seemingly price inquiries.

"How much will you pay for a 1964 Proof Set?"

"Do you sell silver bars? How much are they?"

"I have a coin the size of a half dollar with a horse on it. What's it worth?"

These are typical. But care must be taken in answering them. Later the proof set is brought in but the coins have been neatly placed in a metal container. Silver has shot up 59 cents an ounce since the inquiry concerning the bars. The owner of the "horse coin" refuses to bring it in, declaring he "does not have the time."

Since it is so often a mistake to answer questions over the phone, especially those concerning price, most any dealer will invite you to come into his shop. There can be slight differences in the condition of even a 1964 Proof Set. There is nothing gained in explaining later that the coins in the set are scratched and, therefore, worth far less than the $12 originally offered.

The silver bullion customer might better have the dynamics of the metals markets explained to her so as not to be disappointed by daily or even hourly price changes.

"Horse coin" questions may be well-intentioned, but are often insensitive to even the barest concerns of etiquette.

Don't blame the dealer who is emphatic about wanting to "see it." It's his only defense. A mark of a genuine offer to sell a coin is to have brought it in. The one person every dealer appreciates is someone who makes it clear that he realizes the dealer's time is at least as important as his own.

So, if you have decided to dispose of those duplicates how should you handle it? First call and make an appointment. Put together an inventory of what you wish to sell. A dealer may have no particular interest in what you have for sale. A glance at the inventory can save everyone's time.

Further, unless your intention is to sell the group of coins piecemeal, the question may arise as to what you want for the lot. If you have put together a total of the average retail prices of the coins then at least both buyer and seller have a place to start.

But now here is where things may get difficult. Whether you are paying for an appraisal or not, any offer made by the dealer has a value. It is worth something. For example, in negotiating a price with another buyer, it provides a degree of knowledge that would not otherwise be there. The seller can now deal from somewhat more a position of strength.

Consequently, many dealers are loathe to make an outright offer. Dealers rightly believe that should the seller decline this offer and then seek another, the chance to buy the collection will be lost. The next offer may top the original by some negligible amount. Some dealers respond to this by asking the seller to get several offers and then return. Sometimes it is to the dealer's advantage to make the last offer or at least have the opportunity to top any offers.

Another response on the part of the dealer may be to inquire as to what "ballpark" figure the collector has in mind. This can be a specific amount or percentage of retail. At least now the buyer will have an idea as to whether further discussion is worthwhile. Then too if the two parties are far apart, the dealer has not had to make an offer that proved offensive or ridiculous to the seller.

The situation is complicated when, as often happens, the seller is quite ignorant about the coins he wishes to sell. My advice here is two-part: (1) Ask a disinterested coin collecting party whether the collection or accumulation is worth an appraisal. (2) Assuming the answer is "yes," inquire as to respected dealers in the area and arrange for an appraisal only, as opposed to an offer.

APPRAISED VALUE AND WORTH

An appraisal can be done on an hourly basis or as a percentage of the appraised price. I would expect to pay $20+/hour or anywhere from 2%-5% of the appraised value. Make it clear that you wish to know realistic retail prices. Sometimes an appraisal for insurance purposes can be substantially inflated since in such a case the intention will be to cover all possible replacement costs in full.

Now armed with an appraisal, the seller is not as quite at the mercy of any potential buyer. The "ballpark" figure can be given with some confidence.

And here the seller might expect to receive something around 65-75% of retail for an intermediate level collection, somewhat more for a specialty collection, up to 90%+ of retail if the group consists mainly of bullion coins. Damaged coins, of course, may sell for only a small fraction of their retail price, if at all.

SELLING AT AUCTION

Another avenue for disposing of a collection is through an auction. This method does not, however, shift all decision-making away from the seller. Most auction houses want lots that cannot easily be purchased anywhere else. Of course, these are just the sorts of items that usually make up only a small part of most collections. Run-of-the-mill items will be lumped together in "wholesale" lots, provided the auction house wants them at all.

On the other hand, truly rare items or coins in extraordinarily high grades should probably not be sold anywhere else but at an auction—especially where the seller is ignorant of the market. In such an arena the seller can be virtually guaranteed that the prices realized will be competitive. This is extremely important when condition is so critical in determining price. One "nice" uncirculated Standing Liberty quarter can be worth $150; another $2,500. The uneducated eye certainly cannot see the difference. Now the auctioneer and all those potential bidders make independent assessments. Their joint decision cannot help but be very close to the true condition/value of the coin.

As a seller at an auction, you can expect to receive the price realized on any lot less a 10% commission to the auction house. On very large groups or expensive rarities the commission can be negotiated. I have even seen consignments accepted for 0% commission. In these cases the firm conducting the auction is willing to forego the commission from the seller because that received from the buyer alone makes selling the coin worthwhile.

It is also not uncommon for an auction house to advance the seller a portion of the estimated value of the coins consigned. Then again, months can often go by between the time the coins are sent and the time when a final settlement is made.

The consignor should make himself very aware of the specific terms of the auction house, and there are considerable differences among them. Also, this may not be the preferred method of selling if quick payment is needed.

BUY ADS

A somewhat trickier method by which to sell coins is through the buy ads in collector papers and magazines. In some cases these ads are extensive and list prices and conditions wanted on a variety of different coins. At the very least, familiarizing oneself with these prices will give a seller a good idea about what coins are being sought and the range of prices offered.

Such sources provide an outlet for quantities of similar coins that often make up an accumulation. A local dealer cannot always use multiples of the same issue.

Dealing by mail is however associated with a bit of apprehension. I do not recommend large initial shipments to buyers working out of a post office box. Better to gradually get a feel for the grading standards and dollar limits of the person at the other end. Many ads reserve the right to limit quantities. Others state that "overgraded coins will be returned at the sender's expense."

As a matter of practice, buyers of this sort are not always happy to receive lists of inventories to evaluate. Nor do they take kindly to a sender's demand to buy all or nothing from a shipment.

Do not be surprised should part of the shipment be returned and only a few of the invoiced coins have been purchased. In such a case you must decide if the buyer is engaging in a practice called "cherry picking," where only the coins at the high end of a grading range have been selected; or whether it is truly the case that those returned were overgraded and/or the buyer received too great a response from the ad and is now overstocked on some issues.

Only after dealing for a time in this way will you get a feel for the integrity or idiosyncrasies of the buyer. This method of selling coins would be more appropriate for a collector who intends to sell over a number of transactions. The one-time seller will be "shooting in the dark" with unhappy results.

Buy prices must be regarded by the collector as ephemeral. They represent a price that a buyer is willing to pay at some given period of time. Weeks pass before the ad appears in print. Financial positions change.

I think it always makes sense to give the advertiser a preliminary call. Ask questions about when payment can be expected, what quantities are being sought, what other items are needed. A $2 call can go a long way toward preventing the inevitable anxiety that arises when you've heard nothing three weeks after making a shipment.

Also, follow the normal good practices of securely wrapping the package. Remember coins are heavy and extra precautions should be taken. Include a copy of an invoice. Fully insure or register the package (see our earlier discussion in Chapter 13 for mailing costs).

Undoubtedly it is aggravating to send coins in the mail and then weeks later receive most of them back with counteroffers. But the same sort of things can happen face to face with a dealer. I believe the best attitude to have is that if you think coin "X" is really worth $8 then there is no reason to take less for it. A buyer will certainly be discovered.

Advertised buy offers do tend to raise expectations since something like an actual price is being quoted. Maybe that is why a mail deal gone sour can be so upsetting.

OTHER COLLECTORS

Some success is achievable by offering coins to collector friends, relatives, and club members. However, they may be willing to purchase only coins within their collecting interests. And too, they are less likely to be in a cash position necessary for the purchase of a large collection or individual rarities.

15
Hobby Or Investment

HISTORY AND AESTHETICS

Some suggest that sooner or later every serious collector has to face up to the fact that his collection represents some considerable wealth. As the years go by, a casual inventory of a collection or accumulation can produce surprising results. Even if the coins purchased are able to be sold at only 65% of the price paid, putting aside any modest appreciation, your collection may be worth something in the thousands of dollars.

Although there is a tendency to ignore this accumulated wealth, it is nevertheless clear that the time can soon come when the collection must be understood as some sort of investment. Such a realization need not diminish the enjoyment that coin collecting brings. However, coin collecting is unlike other hobbies where the monies paid out are rarely recovered.

A photography enthusiast usually has no expectation of selling his photos, and, therefore, is even less concerned about any possible appreciation in the value of his productions. People who build and fly radio-controlled airplanes probably never sell at a profit. A more realistic expectation is that their work of several months will be destroyed on the runway someday.

Coins are different. The supply is fixed or diminishing. And the presumption is that with new collectors the demand for many coins will increase.

Since my own introduction to collecting in the early 1960s many "booms" and "busts" have taken place in the market. I can remember when uncirculated rolls of 1950D five-cent pieces were selling for $1,000. Now a roll might sell for $400. I can recall buying nice uncirculated Liberty nickels for $15 each and selling them 15 years later at $150 each.

Different series can be popular for years and then it seems almost as if no one is interested in them. Lincoln pennies, silver dollars, and gold coins have all experienced times when they were "hot" and times when they were "not."

The average collector may well pay little attention to such trends. And if one's collecting interests do not extend to uncirculated coins or coins costing over $50 or so, probably no great price is paid for being oblivious to the possible investment angle to coin collecting.

But, then, too, part of the joy of collecting can be found in selling coins at a profit. Since the 1960s, pressure has come from a variety of sources to treat coin investing as somehow analogous to the stock market. *Coin World* and many other publications and newsletters now have quite extensive coin "trends" sections. Some endeavors are made to plot individual price increases and decreases over as short a period as a week. Excellent books now exist on treating coins as long term investments much as one would buy real estate (see, for example, the Q. David Bowers book mentioned in Chapter 12).

Investment fever is not an uncommon phenomenon. Buying an extra roll or two of an item that is perceived as "underpriced" in the market is one response. And should the retail price of these items shoot up, the effect is seductive. Price appreciation can easily become the entire goal of one's collecting interests.

To avoid reducing coin collecting to nothing but dollars and cents, an effort should be made to see the coins in one's collection for their historical and aesthetic significance.

Interesting historical questions might include researching the various changes in the metal content of certain denominations. Why was the alloy for the Lincoln cent and Jefferson nickel changed during World War II? Was it a necessary change? Why did the Trade Dollar contain more silver than a regular silver dollar? Why are little chop marks often found on these coins?

Why do some coins have arrows next to the date? Why were weird denominations like three-cent and twenty-cent pieces minted? Why were no gold coins minted for circulation after 1933?

Coins can be viewed as miniature sculptures in limited editions. The sheer beauty of a lightly toned uncirculated Liberty Standing quarter can be breathtaking.

Studying a coin closely can bring to one's attention design features never really noticed. Studying the different patterns considered can give one an insight into the reasons for the design that an engraver finally selected.

An even closer inspection of a coin can often give clues concerning the conditions under which it was struck. Had the die cracked or been damaged in some other way? Had it been re-engraved as a shortcut in the striking process? Many coins have one date engraved over another.

Again certain metals seem to function as better mediums for the striking of the details of an engraving. Our recent clad coins appear dull and flat even before they can be circulated. They pale in comparison to high grade Barber coins. They make even a Franklin half dollar look like Michaelangelo's *David*.

An appreciation of these sorts of considerations provides a depth to one's collecting interests. The question, "How much is it worth?" can be considered superfluous.

A PEEK AT THE HISTORY OF COIN PRICE APPRECIATION

On the other hand, I do not wish to disparage the investment/speculation side to coins. This aspect may well be more easily abused and indeed for the average collector realizing a profit over and above that of more orthodox investments is undoubtedly difficult. But I will not deny that money can be made by the wise and patient.

In 1962 I convinced my father to lend me $500 to "prove" that coins were a good investment. He agreed and I promptly spent the entire amount on my next trip to my local coin shop. I recall purchasing, among others, an 1885 and 1886 five-cent piece in uncirculated condition for $140 and $80 respectively.

I held the coins until the early 1970s and sold them for a reasonable profit of something around triple what I had paid. Not too bad, all things considered. The inflation rate was low in those years, so few investment vehicles fared better over that time span.

During those middle 1960s, I, like everyone else, put away silver coins as they began to disappear from circulation (the psychological forces of the era were irresistible). Most of these I still possess. Let's say I saved $200 face in Washington quarters in 1967. And that I paid $300 for them. What would they have to be worth for me now to sell at a real profit? Real is defined as something beyond the rate of inflation. Would I have been better off in Series E Savings Bonds?

Well, if I were to sell today, 23 years later, I would expect to realize 4.5 times face value on the coins, or about $900. The Consumer Price Index now stands at 347.40, 1967 being the base year. To have grown as fast as inflation that $300 would have to be worth $1,050 now. Certainly, other investments have done worse and some better. And there were probably shorter periods of time over which I could have done a lot better in silver. But the point is that silver bullion coins have not been any easy path to riches. Accurately predicting price fluctuations is especially difficult if not impossible.

As I look back, many coins, especially the most easily acquired, the ones that probably form the nucleus of most accumulations, have not done particularly well over the years. Unless one is able to anticipate significant commodity price changes, the prospect of making money in ordinary obsolete coinage is remote.

On the other hand, assuming the ability to grade uncirculated coins and an access to coins that are truly rare, we may well have another matter.

The chart found below attempts to plot price changes of several typical coins over the years.

1. Large Cent F (Coronet type coin)
2. 1909S Lincoln Cent F
3. Liberty Nickel BU (Type coin)
4. 1950D Nickel BU
5. 1916D Dime G
6. 1796 Quarter G (Type coin)
7. Bust Half F (Type coin)
8. Trade Dollar XF (Type coin)
9. 1895P Morgan Dollar PR
10. $1 Gold VF (Type 1)
11. $20 Saint-Gaudens XF-AU (Type coin)
12. Isabella Quarter MS60
13. 1950 Proof Set PR60

The chart below sets out the value of each of these coins for the years 1962, 1975, 1988. These years were within relatively stable periods for the coin market and give us, therefore, a reasonably accurate picture of how an investment might have performed over the past 25 years. The above coins were selected as a representative selection, with the exception of the 1895P Morgan dollar and the 1796 quarter, that would turn up in the average person's collection.

Coin	1962	1975	1988
Large Cent F	$2.00	$5.00	$7.00
1909S Lincoln Cent F	12.00	20.00	50.00
Liberty Nickel MS60	10.00	45.00	125.00
1950D Nickel MS60	5.00	9.00	8.00
1916D Dime G	40.00	80.00	325.00
1796 Quarter G	300.00	750.00	3100.00
Bust Half F	4.00	20.00	35.00
Trade Dollar XF	12.00	70.00	150.00
1895P Morgan Dollar PR	850.00	6000.00	15000.00
$1 Gold VF	25.00	100.00	150.00
$20 Saint-Gaudens XF-AU	50.00	300.00	550.00
Isabella Quarter MS60	40.00	175.00	500.00
1950 Proof Set PR60	55.00	115.00	525.00
Totals	$1405.00	$7689.00	$20525.00

Even if one were to assume a return of 75% of the above amount after commissions, etc., the original investment would have increased by roughly 10 times. If one were to remove the two most expensive items the investment would still have increased by 6 times. What other investments have performed so well!

Like paintings, stamps, baseball cards, and other collectibles, part of the allure of coin collecting will entail the prospect of profit. In the past 20 years any number of firms, some reputable, many not, have played on such hopes.

The promise of fantastic profits can always be established by looking selectively at the past. Indeed, some coins have done very well over the years. Logically, there is nothing that necessitates that this will continue to happen. The forces are largely psychological and, consequently, quite unpredictable.

One need only look at what happened to coin and metal prices in the wake of the stock market "crash" on October 19, 1987. Historically, hard assets have often leaped in value given uncertainty in financial assets. But now, over a year later, the drop in the market has not appreciably affected coin or bullion prices. If anything, both are somewhat lower.

My experience has been that those who come to coin collecting primarily as an investment vehicle soon leave greatly disappointed. They are preyed upon by investment promoters, take shortcuts instead of learning how to grade coins, and in virtually every case, leave the hobby in disgust.

Even for the proficient and wary, investing in coins is full of minefields. Several years ago, the American Numismatic Association Certification Service drastically revised its grading standards, especially for uncirculated grades. And, of course, the standards were toughened, leaving many who had purchased supposedly MS65 coins holding very expensive MS63s.

Even now, when a coin is purchased which is certified as to its grade, the purchaser will do well to act with care. The year it was graded is a factor for deciding how it might currently be graded and priced. For example, some dealers advertise to buy 1982 ANA graded coins at 50% of what they will pay for those graded in 1986.

Such a change in direction does nothing if not shake the confidence of those who primarily hope to profit from the coins they have acquired. It also points up that grading is at its foundations an art not a science, and worse, an art dependent upon the supply and demand forces in the market.

When demand is high and the market is bullish the tendency is to push the limits of previous grading conventions. When a buyer's market returns, prices fall and standards rise.

One beneficial role that investors play in the market is setting aside rolls, even bags, of current coinage for future generations. Unless there had been someone with an eye toward investment it is doubtful that we now could enjoy the variety of well-preserved coins at today's reasonable prices. If anything, over the long run, investors probably keep the prices of coins down.

COIN INVESTMENT AS A HEDGE

During the period 1977-1980, at which time the country was experiencing significant inflation, a huge run up in the price of gold and silver took place, and many predictions were made concerning the total collapse of financial markets.

Some suggested that silver and gold in coin form should be made a part of any thinking person's portfolio as a hedge against disaster.

In this scenario, paper money would quickly become worthless. The image of wagons of Marks, circa 1923, was useful. Bartering, initially at least, would be difficult since communications would be poor or non-existent. Consequently, what was needed was a reliable, negotiable, small unit of real value. Presumably gold and silver bars would need assaying. Obsolete 90% silver coins would become the perfect vehicle. A hedge against disaster.

To some this plan made sense, although planning for such an eventuality will have, by now, over 10 years later, involved considerable cost.

Decision making in this area is reminiscent of good science fiction. I suppose the best one could do would be to make a reasonable estimate of the probability of a disaster of this magnitude. Then apply that probability in percentage terms to one's own wealth and security quotient.

For example, if one thought the chances of financial collapse were something on the order of 5% over the next five years, then putting 5% of one's assets into disaster oriented "real" assets would seem appropriate. A one-year's food supply, a shotgun and shells, 100 cords of wood, and $500 face in Roosevelt dimes might be bought in for simple peace of mind.

But do coins make sense as a hedge in more normal times? My answer would be "yes," but only if I were speaking of a very astute buyer. This buyer would certainly have to know how to accurately grade coins. He or she would almost as certainly have to be able to make purchases at or near wholesale levels. Knowledge of the marketplace would be helpful but not an absolute necessity.

Coins, especially rare ones, can at times present a liquidity problem. They do not trade as easily as stocks and bonds due partly to their individual uniqueness. A buyer must be sought out. Even then prices are usually negotiated.

But for an investor willing to be patient and able to avoid any pressure for quick liquidation, coins provide an interesting but not easy alternative to more traditional and orthodox investments.

The easier path to coin investment, and a much more precarious one is to turn over the decision-making process to a reputable coin dealer/investment advisor. The commissions charged with this approach are considerable. Breaking even, that is, price appreciation in an amount equal to the purchase charges, may take several years (sales taxes present an additional hurdle to profit realization).

And remember all this is said within the context of reliance on a dealer's reputation. If one peruses the advertisers of 1963, very few names survive.

Further, most dealers are automatically in a conflict of interest situation. It is easier to tout coins that can be acquired relatively easily rather than attempt to buy for one's clients coins that are always in short supply.

And when you think of it, if any person, dealer or otherwise, really was convinced that a coin were going to perform extremely well over the next five to 10 years, why would he sell it? That unwillingness to take anything like the risk that the client is asked to take makes any advice rather suspect.

16
Sources of Knowledge

This chapter provides the reader easy access to the acquisition of numismatic information.

1. Coin Papers and Magazines

COINage Magazine
2660 E. Main St.
Ventura, CA 93003

Coins Magazine
Iola, WI 54990

Coin World
P.O. Box 150
Sidney, OH 45367

Hobbies Magazine
1106 S. Michigan Ave.
Chicago, IL 60605

Legacy
311 Market St.
Third Floor
Dallas, TX 75202-9990

Numismatic News Weekly
Iola, WI 54990

The Numismatist
818 N. Cascade Ave.
Colorado Springs, CO 80903

2. Books—General

American Guide to U.S. Coins. Charles F. French. Simon & Schuster, Inc., New York (1988).

Annual Report of the Director of the Mint. United States Mint, Department of the Treasury, Washington, DC 20220.

Coin Collecting Made Easy: Basic Knowledge for the Coin Collector and Investor. Staff of *Coin World.* Amos Press Inc., Sidney, OH (Fourth printing 1987).

Coin World Almanac. Staff of *Coin World.* Amos Press Inc., Sidney, OH (Fifth edition 1987).

The Catalogue and Encyclopedia of U.S. Coins. Don Taxey. Scott Publishing Co., New York (1976).

A Guide Book of U.S. Coins. R.S. Yeoman. Western Publishing Co., Racine, WI (1988).

The Macmillan Encyclopedic Dictionary of Numismatics. Richard C. Doty. Macmillan Publishing Co., New York (1982).

Numismatic Art in America. Cornelius Vermeule. Belknap Press, Cambridge, MA (1971).

U.S. Coins of Value. Norman Stack. Dell Books, New York (1988).

U.S. Mint and Coinage. Don Taxey. Durst Numismatic Publications, New York (1983).

3. Books—Grading

The Accugrade System. Alan Hager. Accugrade Inc., Greenwich, CT (1986).

Grading Coins: A Collection of Readings. Edited by Richard Bagg and James Jelinski. J. Essex Publications, Portsmouth, NH (1977).

A Guide to Grading United States Coins. Martin R. Brown and John W. Dunn. General Distributors Inc., Denison TX (1980).

NCI Grading Guide. James L. Halperin. Ivy Press, Dallas, TX (1986).

New Photograde. James F. Ruddy. Bowers and Ruddy Galleries, Los Angeles (1972).

Official American Numismatic Association Grading Standards for United States Coins. ANA and Western Publishing Co., Racine WI (1987).

4. Books—Specialized

American Half Cents. Roger S. Cohen. Wigglesworth Ghatt Co., Arlington, VA (1982).

America's Copper Coinage 1783-1857. American Numismatic Association (1985).

The Comprehensive Catalogue and Encyclopedia of U.S. Morgan and Peace Silver Dollars. Leroy C. Van Allen and George Mallis. Arco Publishing Co., New York (1976).

The Early Coins of America. Sylvester S. Crosby. Quarterman Publications, New York (1983, a reprint of a 1875 edition).

Early Half Dollar Varieties. Al C. Overton. Colorado Springs, CO (1970).

The Early Quarters of the United States. A.W. Browning. Sanford J. Durst Numismatic Publications, New York (1977, a reprint of a 1925 edition).

Early United States Dimes: 1796-1937. David J. Davis, and others. John Reich Collectors Society (1984).

The Encyclopedia of United States Silver & Gold Commemorative Coins. Walter Breen and Anthony Swiatek. Arco Publishing Inc. (1981).

Encyclopedia of United States Liberty Seated Dimes. Kamal M. Ahwash. Kamal Press (1977).

The Fantastic 1804 Dollar. Kenneth E. Bressett and Eric P. Newman. Whitman Publishing Co., Racine, WI (1962).

The Morgan and Peace Dollar Textbook. Wayne Miller. Adam Smith Publishing Co., Metairie, LA (1982).

Penny Whimsy. William H. Sheldon. Quarterman Publications Inc., Lawrence, MA (1983, reprint of a 1958 edition).

Standing Liberty Quarters. J.H. Cline. Cline's Rare Coins, Palm Harbor, FL (1986).

United States Copper Cents 1816-1857. Howard R. Newcomb. Quarterman Publications Inc., Lawrence, MA (1981, reprint of a 1944 edition).

United States Copper Coins—An Action Guide to Collectors and Investors. Q. David Bowers. Bowers and Merena Inc., Wolfeboro, NH (1984).

United States Gold Coins, an Illustrated History. Q. David Bowers. Bowers and Ruddy Galleries, Los Angeles (1982).

The United States Half Dimes. Daniel W. Valentine. Quarterman Publications, Lawrence, MA (1975, a reprint of a 1931 edition).

The United States Trade Dollar. John M. Willem. Sanford J. Durst Numismatic Publications, New York (1983, a reprint of a 1959 edition).

The Walking Liberty Half Dollar. Anthony Swiatek. Sanford J. Durst Numismatic Publications, New York (1983).

5. Books—Errors

The Encyclopedia of Double Dies, (2 Vols.). John A. Wexler. Robert C. Wilharm News Printing Co. Inc., Fort Worth, TX (1978 and 1981).

How Error Coins Are Made at the U.S. Mints. Arnold Margolis. Heigh Ho Printing Co., Newbury Park, CA (1981).

Modern Mint Mistakes. Philip Steiner and Michael Zimpfer. Whispering Pines Printing, Indiana (1974-80).

Official Price Guide to Mint Errors and Varieties. Mark Hudgeons. House of Collectibles Inc., Orlando, FL (1985).

The RPM Book. John A. Wexler and Tom Miller. Lonesome John Publishing Co., Newbury Park, CA (1983).

6. Books—Counterfeits

Counterfeit Detection. (2 Vols.) Staff of the American Numismatic Association Certification Service. American Numismatic Association, Colorado Springs, CO (1983 and 1987).

Counterfeits of U.S. Coins. Larry Spanbauer. Service Litho-Print Inc., Oshkosh, WI (1975).

Detecting Counterfeit Coins. (Book 1). John Devine. Heigh Ho Printing Co., Newbury Park, CA (1975).

Detecting Counterfeit Gold Coins. (Book 2). John Devine. Heigh Ho Printing Co., Newbury Park, CA (1977).

7. Books—Investing

The Big Silver Melt. Henry A. Merton. Macmillan Publishing Co., New York (1983).

The Coin Collector's Survival Manual. Scott A. Travers. Arco Publishing Co., New York (1987).

High Profits From Rare Coin Investment. Q. David Bowers. Bowers and Merena Galleries Inc., Wolfeboro, NH (1983).

Investing in Rare Coins. Dennis Steinmetz. Steinmetz Coins and Currency, Lancaster, PA (1981).

The Investor's Guide to United States Coins. Neil S. Berman and Hans M. F. Schulman. Coin & Currency Institute Inc., New York (1986).

The Official Investor's Guide To Gold Coins. Marc Hudgeons. House of Collectibles, New York (1985).

Survive and Win in the Inflationary '80's. Howard J. Ruff. Warner Books, New York (1982).

8. Newsletters

The Coin Dealer Newsletter
Box 11099
Torrance, CA 90510

The Certified Coin Dealer Newsletter
Box 11099
Torrance, CA 90510

There are scores of other newsletters on the market. Often, however, these are put together by firms with coins for sale.

9. Professional Organizations and Associations

The American Numismatic Association
818 N. Cascade Ave.
Colorado Springs, CO 80903

The American Numismatic Society
c/o Secretary of the Society
Broadway Between 155th and 156 Streets
New York, NY 10032

Central States Numismatic Society
P.O. Box 223
Hiawatha, IA 52233

Combined Organization of Numismatic
Error Collectors of America
Route 2, Box 6
Andover, SD 57422

Industry Council for Tangible Assets
25 E. St. N.W. Eighth Floor
Washington, DC 20001

Liberty Seated Collectors Club
5718 King Arthur Drive
Kettering, OH 45429

New England Numismatic Association
P.O. Box 99
West Roxbury, MA 02132

Numismatic Literary Guild
P.O. Box 970218
Miami, FL 33197

Pacific Coast Numismatic Society
610 Arlington Ave.
Berkeley, CA 94707

Professional Numismatists Guild, Inc.
P.O. Box 430
Van Nuys, CA 91408

Society of Philatelists and Numismatists
1929 Millis St.
Montebello, CA 90640

Society for U.S. Commemorative Coins
912 Bob Wallace Ave.
Huntsville, AL 35801

10. Grading and Authentication Services

Accugrade
P.O. Box 4304
Greenwich, CT 06830

ANACS
818 N. Cascade Ave.
Colorado Springs, CO 80903-3279

NCI
311 Market St.
Dallas, TX 75202

Numismatic Guarantee Corporation of America
P.O. Box 1776
Parsippany, NJ 07054

Professional Coin Grading Service
P.O. Box 9458
Newport Beach, CA 92658

17
Counterfeit Coins

Collectors and dealers sooner or later encounter counterfeit coins. Two kinds exist. One is made for circulation and intended to cheat the public. Coins of this sort are very crudely made usually from base metals and will more likely be higher denomination coins. You can realize that it would hardly be worthwhile to go to the trouble of illegally reproducing coins of lesser value.

In 30 years of sorting through coins from circulation I have only encountered two or three pieces that were counterfeits of this sort. My view would be that such coins are so seldom seen that they probably have some value as curiosities. I would think it silly to spend them. Having several specimens as examples is worth more than any monetary loss one would suffer for having accepted them.

Both ways of producing counterfeits of this sort are readily detectable. One process is to cast the coin by taking an impression of the genuine one and using that as a mold. This counterfeit has a soapy feeling, and under a ten-power magnifying glass you can see pit marks made by air bubbles.

The second process is to produce an electrotype, made by taking an electrolytic impression of both sides of the coin. The counterfeiter then has two shells which are glued together with a base metal in the hollow center. The type of counterfeit is detectable by the false ring which the fake coin usually has. Unless the job is very skillfully done, you can also see a line around the edge of the coin where the two halves were joined.

The other kind of counterfeit is intended to cheat collectors. These usually involve altering genuine coins. For example, should one be able to successfully remove the "D" mint mark from a 1922D cent, the coin might be passable for the much rarer 1922 cent produced without a mint mark due to a defective die.

Other coins can be altered by adding a mint mark. The 1909S VDB is a notorious example. And any collector should be careful in purchasing one.

With sophisticated minting facilities, coins of even moderate numismatic value have in the past and are currently being produced in order to dupe collectors. Purchasing gold coins has become something of a nightmare. Such coins as the $5 Indian have an incused design making them relatively easy to reproduce. Many gold coins are found in finenesses matching the genuine article. Thus the whole idea is to cheat the person willing to pay above the gold content value of the coin. The face value of these counterfeits is, of course, well below the gold value. When these coins were circulating there was little incentive to counterfeit them. Rather one was more likely then to encounter a gold-plated Liberty nickel dated 1883 without "Cents." A change was made that year to place "Cents" on the coin so as to preclude a gold-plated version being passed for a genuine $5.00 gold piece.

Only experience will give you the ability to detect counterfeits. I do not mind saying that I have been fooled. After all, the counterfeiter keeps up on the state of the art and in some ways has a greater incentive to keep his skills honed. In the near future it is not inconceivable that the quality of the product could surpass that of the genuine article if predatory foreign mints are permitted to operate with no restrictions. Such attempts have already been alleged.

Biography

The author began collecting coins in 1960. Since 1966 he has been selling coins by mail order and setting up at various coin shows in Indiana, Ohio and New York. He has been a dealer in both coins and stamps since 1971, is a member of both the American Numismatic Association and American Philatelic Society, and has written a number of articles on hobby dealer ethics.

Roderick Hughes is also an Associate Professor of Philosophy and Logic at St. Bonaventure University and has been a member of the faculty since 1970.

Glossary

Base Metal—Metal other than precious metal (silver, gold, platinum) used to manufacture coins.

Blank—A planchet that has been further prepared for the coining process.

Braided Hair Type—Middle 19th century type where hair of Liberty is worn up in braids.

Bullion Coin—A coin minted more for the exchange of units of precious metal than for the purposes of commerce.

Bust Type—Showing only the head and shoulder of a figure.

Cameo Proof—A proof coin where the contrast between the design and field is so remarkable that the design often appears to stand out as if on a black background.

Clad—Recent coinage, since 1965, composed of copper and nickel in a sandwich fashion such that the nickel gives the coin a silvery appearance somewhat like previous silver coinage it was meant to replace.

Classic Head Type—A style of the bust of Liberty used in the early 19th century.

Coin—A piece of metal with a design and legend, intended for use as money.

Common Type—Refers to the least expensive date of a particular design.

Commemorative—A special coin, celebrating a person, place or event.

Condition—Usually refers to the amount of wear or absence of wear a coin has had. Also may take into account any damage or special eye appeal a coin may have.

Coronet Type—A style of bust of Liberty used in the early to mid 19th century.

Die—The form from which coins are struck.

Draped Bust Type—An early Liberty type where the bust is covered with a loosely fitting gown.

Field—The background behind the principal figure in a coin design.

Fineness—The proportion of precious metal to base metal in a coin.

Flowing Hair Type—An early Liberty type coin where the hair is not braided or covered.

Fractional Currency—Paper money issued in amounts less than one dollar.

Inscription—All lettering that appears on either the obverse or reverse of a coin.

Impaired—Referring to a proof coin that has seen wear.

Junk Value—The precious metal value or melt value of a coin that has no particular numismatic or collector value. See Chapter 5 for a discussion of various kinds of value.

Lettered edge—Inscription on the edge of a coin. Found especially on our early coinage prior to the use of reeding.

Liberty Cap—A bust of Liberty wearing a distinctive cap.

Liberty Seated—An allegorical figure of Liberty seated, used on our coinage throughout the middle portions of the 19th century.

Liberty Standing—An allegorical figure of the Goddess of Liberty standing, found on the quarter dollar of 1916-1930.

Liberty Walking—An allegorical figure of the Goddess of Liberty walking, found on the half dollar of 1916-1947.

Medal—A metal piece with no legal tender status used to commemorate some person, place, or event.

Milled edge—Parallel vertical ridges around the edge of a coin called reeds.

Mintage—The number of coins produced in a specified period of time.

Mint Error—Any of a variety of mistakes made by the mint in the production of a coin. See Chapter 4 for types.

Mint mark—Small letters placed on a coin to show the place of mintage.

Mint Set—A group of coins of a given year specially packaged or struck for collectors by the Mint.

Numismatics—The science or study of coins and coin collecting.

Obverse—Front of a coin, the side having the principal design feature. Also referred to as the "heads" side of the coin.

Overdate—Coin made from an altered die, showing traces of a different date.

Pattern—Experimental coin struck to experiment with different metals or designs.

Planchet—The blank piece of metal on which a coin design is stamped or struck.

Proof—Condition of a coin struck from a polished die, often giving the coin a mirror-like appearance.

Proof Set—A group of coins of a given year specially struck and packaged by the mint under the conditions mentioned above.

Relief—The relation of the design of the coin to the field. Bas-relief means the design features are raised with reference to the field. An incused design means the design features are below the field or recessed.

Reverse—The side opposite the principal design feature. Also referred to as the "tails" side of the coin.

Restrike—A coin made at a later date from an original die.

Symbols—Small additions to the design supplementing the main subject.

Token—A private coin-like piece made for advertising or propaganda purposes.

Type—The kind of coin as designated by the principal design.

Varieties—Minor variations in coins, such as size of letters, size of date, added dot, different metal content, etc.

737.4973
FEL

Fell's United
States coin book

$14.95   10273

DATE		

© THE BAKER & TAYLOR CO.